# THE OMAR HOWARD STORY

Written by Omar Howard

 **Ordering Information:**

Quantity sales: Special discounts are available on quantity purchases by corporations, associations, and others. For details, contact the publisher at the address above.

Orders by U.S. trade bookstores and wholesalers:

Please contact Freedom is a Choice, Inc.

Visit: www.freedomisachoice.net

Email: freedomisachoice2012@gmail.com

Social Media:

Facebook -www.facebook.com/freedomisachoice.net/

Instagram- @omar_howard

Twitter - @howard_omar

Printed in the United States of America

ISBN-13: 978-1548089238

ISBN-10: 1548089230

## Acknowledgements

To my beautiful mother Christine Howard and my stepfather Ricky Collins. There can never be enough words to say thank you for standing by me through the dark periods in my life.

To my son Deshon, you have truly been my inspiration to become the best man I can be. I want to also dedicate this to my grandparents and immediate family members whom I hold dear to my heart. I dedicate this book to three distinguished men who helped me to become the man that I am today: Chaplain Climen Nix, Mr. Ed Menifee, and Warden Stanley Arrington.

To my support team: my sister Andrea Shelton, The HeartBound Ministries family, Dexter Hull, Jeffrey Whitten, the Hancock family, The Johnson family, The Springfield Baptist Church family and all my friends that have supported me and have been through the struggle.

To everyone that has played a part in my evolution from a child to a man, I dedicate this to you.

# TABLE OF CONTENTS

# INTRODUCTION

It's all in a name:

Omar – (Hebrew/Arabic) eloquent gifted speaker.

Sheehan – (Irish) peaceful one.

Howard – (Old English/Scandinavian) Noble Watchman

I look over my life and I see so many ups and downs. So many times I wanted to simply give up. The same question always comes to mind, "Why me?" My life has been an interesting journey. Let me add, if I had a choice, it's a life I wouldn't have chosen. Then as I read through the Bible I realize that no king, prophet, judge, apostle, or disciple went through life without some great trial or struggle that they had to overcome. I'm pretty sure they probably asked, "Why me?" as well. The Bible is full of stories to show the low and highs of great men and women of God who went through trial upon trial that made them become the people we still read about today. Yet my remains, "Why me?" Why did I have to deal with all of these trials? Why did I have to grow up like this? Why God? Why? But, through it all, as I take you down this journey of my life the same question that you may asked God he answered many years ago for me. That question is, why not you? Maybe that is your answer as well.

I was born November 8th, 1974 to Christine Howard in New York, in the borough of Manhattan. My mother and Aunt Eugene, or Be-Be as we called her, raised me. Be-Be was the one who helped give me my name. I was told that they were looking through a Muslim book when Omar jumped out at them.

For the next year or so I stayed in New York with my Aunt Be-Be, who told my mom to go back to Alabama to finish up school. The story, as I was told, was that my mom was in high school and very involved her senior year. She was in a lot of different activities: cheerleader, prom queen, pageants, etc. She eventually ventured out and met an Auburn University basketball star, William Wallace in 1973. Well, of course, one thing led to another and I was born. You would probably ask as you read through my life why I never meet him. Well, I don't know either but, my mom said it wasn't planned, and it wasn't a choice. Now my mother, who for the most part, had a great life with all that she was doing and involved in, let the fear of letting my grandmother know she was pregnant caused her to flee to New York. My mother eventually moved back to Alabama to finish up school and left me with my aunt until she was ready to tell my grandmother she had a son.

After one in a series of events, where my Aunt Be-Be stole money from a neighborhood drug dealer and he threatened to hurt us both for her actions, my aunt figured it was time for me to go to Auburn, Alabama. It was now time for the rest of the world to be introduced to Omar Sheehan Howard.

# THE HOWARDS

My family consisted of my grandfather, Willie Howard, who was illiterate, yet a master electrician, farmer and hunter. Granddad was also a heavy drinker, and during the times I stayed with him, a very loving family man who loved me unconditionally. The one memory that still has a powerful impression on me was that in spite of coming home drunk most of the time, every night he was down on his knees praying for hours. What I admired most about him was that with all his faults, troubles and struggles, he knew who to turn to.

My grandmother, Mrs. Amaziah Howard, was the matriarch of the family. She played a major part in raising me during my time in Auburn. My grandmother made such an impression in my life. She was the mother of eight, and grandmother to 10. She was a teacher, a fervent volunteer, a comforter and a most assured provider.

We lived on a dirt road right beside a train track in a little grey house with a tin roof. We all lived under one roof: my Aunt Be-Be, my Uncle Charles, my cousin Mark, my cousin Pookie, my Aunt Marion, my Aunt T.C., her daughter Ambriah, my twin cousins Sammy and Carolyn, or Pete Pie as we called her. We also shared space with an extended family of roaches, mice and wood rats! My granddad also had several beagles, and a couple of rabbit dogs.

My mother had moved to Georgia when I was too young to remember. She always came back to Alabama to visit me. She would always surprise me with gifts. That was the highlight of my days when I knew my mom was coming home.

In our house, race was not an issue, and poverty was not a thought. I was just a kid who only wanted to have fun. Life began to shape itself as I was being exposed to a lot of things that I should have been shielded from; as my grandmother probably was trying to do. Not having a father, or brother, or sister, my uncle and cousins played a major role in my upbringing. It was at a very young age that I first had sex with a girl as my cousins looked on and coached me through it. My cousin was like my big brother and major influence in my life. At that time of my life, I was introduced to very negative and bad influences. I wasn't only introduced to sex at a young age, but a series of stealing and other criminal activities.

Those moments turned me into a mannish and thievish young kid. This was the start of a corrupted life style. Now, my Aunt T.C. was one of my favorite aunts. She was very tough and applied 95% of the whoopings I received while I lived in Alabama. She truly loved me though, and surely was a protector. My Uncle Charles was my favorite uncle because he loved me and he was funny, but he was also a thief, liar, hustler, and gigolo. You name it, he was that, but I loved all that about him for some strange reason. My Aunt Be-Be is also Mark's mother. I just loved her, but I observed her go through a lot. Just like most of my family, she was a heavy drinker, and she was always on the move.

I was introduced to a lot of my aunts and uncles' friends. Mark had the most friends that I attached myself to. A few became close friends, but maybe too close for comfort.

There was this one friend of my cousin that had gotten real close to the family and was my cousin's best friend. He was surely someone that we put a lot of trust in, but that trust gave way to dark secrets and hidden agendas he kept in his heart. One night, I was hanging out with my cousin and his best friend. We were standing in front of the abandoned house next to my grandmother's and it was kind of late. It was always fun hanging out with my cousin though, listening to them talk about girls or doing something crazy. My cousin walked off to go into the house for whatever reason and left me and his best friend by ourselves. While we were standing there, his best friend told me to watch him as he pulled out and showed me his private part. Me being only about 5 years old, it puzzled me and fear rushed through me. Then he began to jack off in front of me and told me to watch. He even grabbed my hand to help him while he finished. My heart was filled with fear because even though I was young, I knew it was wrong. But I didn't know to tell my cousin or anybody else about what he just made me do. He told me don't tell no one or I would get in trouble. My cousin Mark was a goodhearted person, but, in a moment he can go to being a very dark hearted person with the capability of killing someone. Those thoughts were in the back of my head being that I've seen him about to kill a guy, and beat him up because this guy took money from me. I knew if I told my cousin he would have surely done something crazy. I did all I could do to avoid him for the next several weeks. Yet every time he came around he would try and get me alone. I was in great fear of him, he eventually stopped bothering me because of my avoidance. I nevertold

17

anyone about this experience and even blocked it out of my mind for years.

My grandma eventually moved out of the little grey house by the tracks and up the street on Martin Luther King Highway. By that time I was going to 4$^{th}$ grade, not knowing this would be my last year in Alabama. The school year ended and summer hit and I got the word that my mother was coming to move me to Georgia. I was very excited until the day I got ready to leave and the reality that I was leaving my grandparents hit me. That had to be one of the saddest days of my life. I had grown attached to my grandparents, and they surely were attached to me. They honestly didn't want to give me up, they really cared about me. That ride from Alabama to Georgia was a long and sad one. I felt like I lost my world when I moved to Georgia.

We moved to a small town on the outskirts of Atlanta called Lithonia into Evan Mills Place Apartments. I was heading in to the 5th grade at Stoneview Elementary.

Lithonia was an interesting place. So many new people, friends, and it also meant me even getting to meet some more of my family. Eventually, some of my relatives from Alabama moved up. My Uncle Charles, my Aunt Re, Cousin Mark, plus my two other cousins moved in this two bedroom apartment with me and my mother.

The problems my mom thought she left in Alabama followed her to Atlanta. The problems that a dysfunctional family brings are like a curse that won't go away. My family was fun to be around, but the negative personalities, the drugs, the drinking, but the fighting was most disturbing. Watching the people that I cared about most, fight each other like they were strangers was terrifying. I loved my family, and for the most part it was nice having them around me. My mother knew she had to move away from the violence and the drug using. I managed to pass 5th grade and met a lot of friends along the way and was having a good time in my new state of Georgia, even though I missed my grandparents.

In the summer of '86, before the start of my 6<sup>th</sup> grade year, my mother moved us in with her boyfriend. This for me, was a strange situation because I've never been in a living situation with my mom and a boyfriend. My 6<sup>th</sup> grade year was truly different with a new school, new friends, and new place to live. This is when things really began to get interesting in my life, when I started school at Clifton Elementary. Being that you're a new kid, you catch a buzz and people are trying to feel you out. I surely got a lot of attention from females, and met a lot of good friends that would be lifelong. My 7th grade year was a moment in life where my interest in girls began to fly through the roof. I dated, flirted, touched, grabbed, and lusted over these new girls that I was meeting. I had a great time that year as we were preparing to graduate and go to high school. My last year in elementary school was very fun.

There were a lot of my mother's boyfriend's relatives that were staying with us. I didn't mind because it kept a lot of humor and excitement in our apartment. Our apartment became a fun house where they played cards and stayed up all night. Plus, a lot of my friends often came over.

The last day elementary school had arrived and I graduated. I was so excited that I was getting ready to head to junior high! We had the ceremony where we received our certificates of graduation. It was happy and sad as we hugged and laughed knowing for some that would be the last time you see them. It was hard to walk away from friends you had spent a lot of time with for the last 2 years. We would get to see each other one more time at a graduation party that would be held later that day. I came home and my family cooked a great meal. I was so elated that I had passed $7^{th}$ grade and was heading to the $8^{th}$ grade. Later that day, I put on my new clothes my mom bought me. My friends and I got together to head over to the party that was being thrown. On our way, one of my closest friends and I begin to play and wrestle as we headed toward the party. We were joking around and I took off running trying not to get caught by him and something suddenly happened. It felt like I was sleeping or something, when I suddenly opened my eyes and realized that I was laying on the ground. For a few minutes, I didn't know what was going on with me. The only two things I saw were a car stopped right in front of me, and one of my friends staring at me, pointing at my leg. When I looked down I could see my bone coming out of my left leg. Immediately pain began to rush through my body and I realized I had been hit by a car. I experienced pain like I never felt before. Since I wasn't too far from my apartment, my friends ran to tell my mother. Before I knew it my, mother, boyfriend and nephew were all around me crying and trying to comfort me. The street suddenly was filled with bystanders and friends from the party. I could hear people crying, telling me it's going to be ok as the ambulance came and they took me to Grady Memorial Hospital. They took me to the emergency room, where they immediately took me into surgery to repair my leg. The doctor said the way I was hit that it was a miracle my leg didn't get torn off, and that they were able to put it back together.

I had to stay in the hospital for two weeks until I had enough strength to walk on crutches or a walker. The day came when I was released from the hospital. For the next 3 months, I was in bed with a full cast on my leg. Being in the bed wasn't all that bad. Actually, I had the best summer of my life. Family and friends poured in all summer long to check on me. Not one day passed that wasn't filled with excitement. It was also that summer that I had sex for the second time in my life. I may have had three girlfriends over the course of the summer of 1988.

That summer also came with tragedy as a close friend of the family, Mike, who used to play the role of big brother and watched me when my mother was gone, passed away. One morning his young brother woke up and said he dreamed that Mike had died. We didn't think much of it, but about three days later that dream came to reality. Someone shot Mike in the head. His brothers came and got me and we jumped in the car to go over to the place where his brother was shot. That was one of the worst feelings I ever felt, and the first time someone close to me died at the hands of violence.

A new chapter started after that summer. I was on my way to junior high school, McNair to be exact. I was excited even though two of my closest friends, Brian and Eric moved and went to Avondale High School. I still had two of my best friends and big brothers, Boyzie and Mike, who were actually going to McNair High School. Not having a biological brother, it was easy for me to attach myself to brothers who had concern for me. I really enjoyed and cherished the time I spent around those two as they begin to shape my character. I honestly tried to duplicate my life around them as they taught me a lot and inspired me to dream.

My mother moved again and I got transferred to Lithonia High School. I was a pretty good student and maintained good conduct and grades throughout my 8$^{th}$ grade year. I started to really enjoy basketball and other sports as well, but basketball was my thing. I was getting better and had made plans to try out for the team the next year when I hit 9$^{th}$ grade.

# IT'S A NEW GAME

My 9th grade year started off well, but I slowly started losing focus. I started skipping school on the regular. My conduct started getting worse and my focus shifted from attending school and playing basketball to being a troublemaker. While in 9th grade, I began to date upper class girls. One I began to date was the introduction to a new game. While visiting her, I was introduced to her brother-in-law, and a host of friends. Some I knew, and some I didn't know. That year, I began to see a lot of guys I knew from Bruce Street involved in this drug game and my attention was roused because I saw money, jewelry, clothes, cars, etc., and I wanted it. The more I saw it, even though I knew it was wrong, the more I wanted the shiny things and the popularity that came with it.

My girlfriend's brother-in-law introduced me to the drug game. The day I was supposed to start, I was anxious and I was scared if my mom would find out. I couldn't wait to get out of school that day to go over there and start my new job selling drugs. When I got to the house, he gave me a bag with 20 rocks of crack cocaine in it. I was going to get $20 off every $100 I sold. At that time in my life, 14 years old, that was a come up for me. I thought it was going to be easy and I was going to sell a lot of dope and make some money. He sent me out there with some other guys that he had rolling for him to the hunter hole down on Bruce Street. That night I was excited because I was ignorant to the true consequences of selling drugs. That included the long nights, the greed, the robbers, and all that came with it. I had been out there for a few hours and sold about 8 rocks when something happened that spooked me. It gave me a quick lesson to how dirty the drug game was, and I needed to learn quickly how to survive. It was about 9:30 PM and we were competing to sell drugs. Lithonia Police pulled up in the trap and it scared me! So I took the 12 crack rocks I had and stashed them under the stairs not knowing anyone was watching. I walked away from all the police lights so I wouldn't get questioned. Twenty minutes passed and the police pulled off and it seemed the coast was clear. I was ready to get the rest of these drugs sold off because I had to be home soon. I got to the stairs and my stomach dropped. Where was my sack? It was gone. Someone had got me. What was I going to do? Who got me for my sack? I was confused. It was my first day and I didn't know how I was going to explain this to my girlfriend's brother. I had to call him and tell him. I was scared. He rushed over there. I didn't know what to expect. To my surprise, he and one of the older guys got out of the car and begin to threaten anyone that may have taken the sack. That lasted about 10 minutes. To my surprise again, someone confessed that their son had stolen the dope and gave me back my sack.

My night was over as he told me to get in the car and we headed toward my house. I surely thought he was disappointed. When he pulled up to the house he smiled and told me I did well. He went into his pocket and pulled out 40 dollars and gave it to me. He told me he would see me tomorrow after I get out of school. I got out the car happy and ready to get back out there.

# THE DOMINO EFFECT

I never knew that only a few bad choices were going to send me down a dark path that I never thought I would be on. The dreams I had of going to college were quickly replaced with dreams of hustling and making fast money. The streets give you false dreams of riches and fame that have dead-end consequences. Young with no guidance, the streets became my father, and the homies became my family. I began to enjoy selling dope and becoming a street hustler. It became easy, to the point all I wanted to do was sell drugs and hang out as much as possible.

Education wasn't important. Respect wasn't important, Staying out all night, going to clubs, strip clubs, fighting, drinking, smoking weed, not realizing I was becoming a product of my environment, were all that mattered. Growing up, I wasn't taught to be hard and ruthless, but the more I played in the streets the more my heart begin to harden and emotions weren't a factor, only survival. The more I entertained the streets, the more I began to conform to the evils of living the street life of selling drugs, breaking in cars, stealing cars, and breaking in houses. You name it, I tried it. Along this dark path, there was a glimpse of light that made me want to change. Quickly as it came, it left without a trace.

The year of 1990 was the beginning of a lifestyle that I wasn't expecting. Along with hustling, some friends and I went out to get in to some mischief. We skipped school and we drove to different high schools with the intentions of jumping guys and taking Starter jackets, shoes, hats, or whatever. My closest friend led the charge, always throwing the first punch. We ended up going to four high schools. The last one was Stone Mountain High School. We drove around the school looking for students with Starter jackets on. We saw some kids walking, a few boys and a few girls. We drove down to the gas station at the end of the street and got out to walk back and confront the guys who had on the Starter jackets. Once again, my best friend led the charge. He began to throw punches at one of the guys as the rest of us charged the other guys to take their jackets. We succeeded in taking the jackets. We ran back to the car, jumped in, and headed back to our apartment. It was four of us in the car; we took about 6 Starter jackets that day. We arrived at the apartments with excitement, not knowing that this day was the beginning of a cycle of trouble. When we arrived at Meadow Woods Apartments, we were met with a parade of police cars. Blue lights were everywhere. We were taken out of the car and put into the police car. At that moment in our life, we still kind of took it as a joke. We cursed the police officer that transported us to the police station. We even went as far as singing f*** the police song that was popular by the most influential rap group at that time, NWA. We sang the whole song and did it all the way to the police station.

When we arrived, they booked us, questioned us, and then sent us to juvenile. My best friend and I were sent to DeKalb Youth Detention Center (DYDC). The other guys were sent to different regional youth detention centers (RYDC) until we were given bond. This was my first time being in any serious trouble, and this was the first time really praying to God, besides when I used to have terrible nightmares and I would quote Psalms 23. Having to spend several days in juvenile was scary. What should have been a wakeup call became a cycle in and out of custody. This began in 1990. I had run-ins with the law several more times as a juvenile.

The next time I went to RYDC was when I went over to a friend's house after he told me he had two girls over there. I went there because my life was all about money and the girls. To us girls were targets to have sex with, nothing more. I was working at the time with my stepfather doing construction. I was 16, had a girlfriend that I really liked, but didn't know how to be faithful.

I went to Meadow Woods Apartments to my friend's place. Two girls were there. One I knew whom I had been involved with a couple of years earlier. We joked around with the girls and eventually I went into the room with one of the young ladies to become intimate. Once we finished we all joked around until I got ready to leave. I was leaving as other friends of ours came over. I went home because I had to be up early the next morning to go to work.

I woke up early and my stepfather and I went to work. We worked about 10 hours that day. I got home tired, hungry and dirty. I was met at the door by my mother with some disturbing news. She told me a DeKalb County detective called and asked to speak to me concerning an accusation that the two young ladies screamed rape on us. My heart dropped to the floor and I gasped, as I couldn't believe that I was being questioned for rape. My mother called the detective and told him she was bringing me up there so he can question me. I took a shower and put on some clothes. We went to DeKalb County and asked for the detective. He took us to the office, or let's say the questioning room. I told him the whole story, and for the first time ever in front of an officer, I told the truth. He wrote everything down and said I appreciate your honesty. They also had my best friend in the other room. He told me unfortunately, I have to charge you with rape and take you to juvenile. I could not believe what I was hearing. I told the truth and I'm getting locked up for something I didn't do.

They sent us to Gainesville, GA RYDC. When we arrived, we couldn't believe that we were in this situation. One of correctional officers told us not to tell people what we were locked up for because they would probably jump on us. Not that we were scared, but we didn't tell anyone. The next three days, all I could do was pray to be out of this situation. We went to court about three days later and were met with some good news from the District Attorney. She said she didn't believe the stories those young ladies told. The D.A made recommendations to the judge to give us a signature bond.

The judge gave us a $500 bond and we had to pay $50. We paid and got out. I was so excited to get out, but I had to figure out how to explain to my girlfriend, who was pregnant at the time, why I was locked up. So, of course, I lied about my involvement. Several weeks later the young ladies told the truth, that they ran away and when their mother found out where they were and popped up to the apartment, they got scared and claimed they were raped. Thank God they told the truth.

You would have thought with all that I've been through in those years that I would have straightened up. I still ask myself everyday where I turned wrong. Yet I still found myself getting in trouble with the same people.

My girlfriend, with my mom's permission, moved in with me. I thought it was pretty cool since we were around each other all the time, but I quickly learned playing house wasn't as fun as I thought it was. It began to get complicated.

# PLAYING HOUSE

I wouldn't imagine having a live-in girlfriend that was pregnant would be so difficult. Me not having a father, brother, or positive role model made it even more difficult. Because of that I didn't have a clue on how to love. I thought because I was having sex with her, I also loved her. I didn't know how to be a father since I never had one of my own. My girlfriend moved in sometime in 1991. We even decided to go to school in Gwinnett, which was kind of fun. I was amazed because for the first time in a long time I was focused and doing my work, passing my classes. The fun part was we didn't have to be in class till 10 AM and we were out of school at 2 PM. For the two semesters we were there, it was fun and exciting. But time passed and money tightened, my girlfriend's stomach was getting bigger, and the pressure was on. We ended up dropping out of school to make some money and prepare for the birth of our son. I hustled selling drugs, but this time I started robbing. There wasn't a day that passed that I wasn't lurking for someone to rob. I started to get addicted to the armed robbery life.

In March of 1992, my son was born, and I tell you, that may have been the best day of my life. It didn't start out so great. A close friend and I were riding around doing what guys do. I was ignoring my beeper because we were at some girl's house being mannish as always. When we left, I finally looked at my pager and it had 911 about 20 times from her cousin's house. I finally called her cousin and she told me my girlfriend was in labor. My heart dropped to the ground. All I could think about was not being there when my son was born! I don't know if I was more scared of missing her have the child, or hearing her scream and shout, probably the latter. I jumped back in the car and my homeboy rushed me to the hospital. I got upstairs and rushed into the emergency room. She seemed to light up with joy knowing her child's father was standing by her side. I could see the tip of his head was coming out as she started squeezing my hand. Suddenly his head popped out and blood shot out. I almost fainted because I thought back to when I got hit by a car and I saw all that blood. It was an amazing site for sure to see my son being born.

When my son arrived in this world I was very excited. I took my son in my arms and turned away from everyone as tears begin to flow out of my eyes. My heart pounded, and for the first time in my life I felt I had something to live for, and something to call my own. When my son was born, I was determined to change my life because I wanted to be a good father to my son. I didn't want my son to be like me and grow up without a father figure. So I stopped selling drugs, along with all the things that I was doing, and enrolled back in school. This was a very exciting time for me. For the first time in years I was trying to do right in school. The assistant principal made a statement that struck me. He said, "This is a good year. Omar is not getting in any trouble!"

I said, "I have a son and I want to be part of his life. I don't want to be like my father. I want to be here for my son."

That truly started to be a good year. I also got a job at McDonald's on Evans Mill Road. I was so excited and felt I was on the right path. Life didn't get easier though, it became more challenging since the fast money wasn't coming in. I allowed myself to be sucked back to the streets. I went back to what was easy, and that was robbing.

That same year tragedy struck. My close friend and play brother, Eric, got killed coming from the club. Then another friend got killed trying to rob someone. That really freaked me out but I kept on robbing whenever I could find a person that had money.

Things got worse towards the end of the year in 1992. I got caught cheating, lost friends to violence, and money wasn't coming in the way I thought it would. I was stressing, depressed, and had become very violent towards my son's mother who was pregnant again. I even became very disrespectful to my mother.

I got through Christmas, and even through the new year of 1993. I had quit my job and started back hustling. My son's mother had moved out because I was being abusive, mentally and physically. I had gone as far as threatening her life. I didn't know what to do with myself. I was lost.

1993 was the year my whole life would forever change. The very person I was determined not to be to my son, I became, just in a different way. The hustle game for me was anything that would bring in money. I started back hanging with some guys who were known robbers, and that began to get out of control. We began to rob whoever we thought had money. We were living recklessly, trying to get rich. People never knew I was robbing, except a few, because I didn't look like a robber. But hanging around these guys was an indication that I either knew what was going on, or that I was a part of this robbing crew. There were still many warnings signs that indicated I was going down the wrong road fast, but I ignored them.

February 3rd was a turning point for me. I never knew that I would be involved in what was about to take place. Two of my closest friends, me, and two other people were in the car looking for a nice robbery to commit. One of the guys said he knew where we could go and get some money. We pulled in to the back of the apartments and all of us got out. My two best friends at the time, a girl and a guy, got out of the car, along with myself. The two older guys stayed at the car. That night, I felt strange for some reason. I didn't feel up to it and I expressed that to one of my friends. He responded by saying just do this for me; you know I don't trust anyone else. Even though I had a bad feeling, I wasn't going to let my friend down. My other friend, the girl, went to knock on the door. Someone opened the door, we could hear the voice of a man, and she was talking to him to distract him. I told my friend to go ahead and draw down on the guy;

we were about 12 feet away. So he proceeded to the door as I stood back and watched. He drew down on the guy at the door. The guy tried to close the door and they began to tussle, and suddenly I heard a gunshot. I ran to the door and pushed my friend to the side because I thought someone was shooting out the door. When I looked down I saw a man lying on the floor with a hole in his head. In that moment, it seemed like an eternity as I looked back at both of my friends like, what in the hell happened. In slow motion, we all took off running. We got to the car and pulled off. It was very quiet for about 5 minutes then questions were flying. We got to one of the other guy's house to drop him off. He told us to give him the gun so he could get rid of it. We were so scared that we didn't give him the gun, which was a mistake.

We drove off to go home and slept on the fact that someone died.

The next day my two best friends and I went to rob another house with the same gun that killed the guy. We even joked about not letting my friend hold the gun because he might accidentally shoot somebody else. Fortunately, the guy didn't come home so we left and went home. The following day I had a very strange dream of robbing a house and the police came to the house. I remember in the dream, going to the window and jumping out of it. All I can recall is that it seemed like a long time for me to hit the ground, and it was so dark that I couldn't see. Suddenly I hit the ground and I jumped up and ran to a fence and all of a sudden I got shot by a police officer. As I was dying, I woke up. This dream had me sweating and tears coming from my eyes and it seemed so real but as I woke I said to myself I'm glad it was a dream.

That Friday night around 9 PM, one of the older guys I hung with called and told me he had a spot to hit, and to let him know what I wanted to do. I was over at my best friend's house at the time with mostly everyone that was at the murder scene. I rode over there with another friend of mine whose mother's car phone was in the car. I called my homeboy and said I'm coming to meet you. He asked who I was coming with and when. I told him and he said he would come get me. I convinced him otherwise. When I got ready to leave my best friend's house, everyone told me not to go. They were bad news. I told them I would be right back, but again they told me not to leave. I told them one more time that I would be back. Not realizing I wasn't coming back.

The night was young, my friend and I went to meet my other homeboys. We arrived at my friend's baby's mother's house around the corner from the house we were going to go in. They grabbed their guns. My homeboy and I got the two guns that were at our other friend's house, one that was used in the murder a couple nights before. We all went over to the house. We walked to the side of the house. As we got prepared to enter the house, I put on my hoodie, but no one else had anything covering their faces. We went to the front door and opened the screen door really quietly.

We sat there for a few minutes as we tried to play with the doorknob. We could see people moving around inside. We were trying to figure out who was going to kick the door open. My adrenaline began to pump. I was getting excited as I always did. While everyone was talking, I told them to come on so we could go in. I went to the door and kicked it in and we all ran in. The energy was real high. Everyone was running around and one of my homies had all three of the women lay down while we searched the house.

We searched for about 5 minutes but didn't find anything. So, one of my homeboys and me walked out the front door. I told him to hold on so I could get the other two guys. I ran back into the house and the guys were still looking around. I started looking around as well, and stumbled up on a locked money bag. I looked for the keys and found them on one of the women's car keys. I grabbed the keys and began to put the key into the locked money bag when suddenly I heard a knock at the front door. I looked out the window and my heart dropped to the ground. There was a police car outside and a policeman knocking at the door. I dropped the bag I had, and told the other guys. We began to panic as we went back and forth to try to find a way out of the house. I ran to the patio door, and for some reason I couldn't get it open. I ran passed the other two and ran to the backroom. I went to the window and opened it up. Not knowing how far the jump was, I leaped with no hesitation. It was pitch dark and it seemed like it took forever to hit the ground. When I finally landed, I jumped up and ran toward the woods. I saw this gate and I ran inside of it, up through the woods and between some houses until I got to the street. Well, rather the cul-de-sac where we parked. My friend's baby's mother's house is where we hid out. Everyone made it back except one of my homeboys. We watched from the window as he was running back and forth. The police were looking for him but he finally got a break and ran across the street. He ran to the back of the house where we let him in.

Now, for the moment we believed we were in the clear. We even fell asleep for about a couple of hours. We were awakened by a knock at the door at about 2:30 AM. We jumped up and were listening as my friend's baby mother's father answered the door. We listened as the police were questioning him about the cars out front of the house. It was a sky-blue Cadillac he knew about, but the Honda coupe he couldn't account for, he had no idea whose it was. The police left and we thought that the night was over.

We fell back asleep for a couple of more hours. Two hours had gone by and I was awakened by my homeboy who I rode over to my other partners' house with. He woke me up and told me it was clear, he was going home. I jumped up put on my shoes, then our other homeboys, the older ones, told us to chill until the shift change. We told them we were about to go home since everything should be clear. At least that's what we thought. We go to the car, and before we get in we hide the gun. We got into the car and headed home. As we get close to end of Marbut Road and Panola Road we see a black Mustang with one headlight come up behind us. My friend pointed out that the car looked familiar as if he had seen it before. When we began to pull off Police started to come from everywhere, with guns drawn. We were snatched out the car we were in and slammed on the police car, shook down, handcuffed and thrown in the back seat of the police car. It felt like I was in the middle of a nightmare as I was hauled off to jail.

I remember being taken to the holding cell. It was dark, cold and lonely. I cried because I couldn't believe I was back in that dreadful place. The detectives came and got me and then began to question me. They asked me about where I was and who was with me. I was acting dumb and wouldn't answer their questions. This went on for hours. They sent several detectives in to talk to me. They even tried to send a black detective in there to talk to me as if that would persuade me, but I was still in denial. They even went on to say I wasn't picked out in the lineup but my other co-defendant was.

They left again for about an hour and I thought I was in the clear. The detectives walked back into the room with a written statement from my co-defendant. He laid down the statement and asked me did I now want to tell the truth. I put my head down because I couldn't believe what I was reading.

He admitted to robbing the house and what type of gun he had used in the robbery. It also said Omar had a big black gun with a long clip on it. I sat there for a few minutes crying trying to figure out what to say. I did what anyone would do, I lied. I went on to say I was drunk and didn't know what he did. I was just with him and I didn't know his friends, I thought we were going to a party. I tried to take myself out of the picture as best I could but it didn't work because they charged me with armed robbery. I learned that day how wicked some of the law enforcement were as he wrote the statement and made me sign it, threatening me about getting me a life sentence. When I got ready to walk out of the room after the questioning, around 8 AM., the detective said something strange. He said that same color jacket was described in a murder at Snapfinger Creste Apartments a few days prior. My heart dropped to the ground as they took me to the booking area. I remember sitting there while the women looked at me and told me I was a handsome young man. They then asked why I would get myself into this kind of trouble. That was painful to hear because my whole life went before my eyes as I reflected on how in the hell I got myself into this. They took my clothes, she finger-printed me, and they booked me.

They took me across the street and put me in the annex part of DeKalb County Jail. I was kind of relieved because the main part of the jail was called the Thunder Dorm. You either had to know someone or just be a standup guy. They put me in my dormitory. The last few times I was incarcerated, I knew I was getting out. But this time I knew I would be gone for a long time. I picked up the phone and dialed my mother and we talked. I remember her saying the she didn't think she can get me out of this one. I told her that I think I'm going to be gone for a long time. We talked and eventually we hung up. I later called my friends that warned me not to go do this and we talked for a while. I went down the list of a few people that I talked to and told them the story. Later that night, under the covers, I cried because I couldn't believe I got myself into this, not even knowing that in a few months it would get more complicated. The days turned into long emotional weeks. The second week I was in there I got a surprise visit from my son's mother who was also pregnant with her second son. To see her sitting in that chair was emotional for me. She told me she knew something was wrong the night I got locked up, my son wouldn't stop crying. We talked and giggled but she said something that would forever prick my soul. She told me I left her out here to raise these kids by herself. That tore my soul out, seriously. I felt like the scum of the Earth. I thought about two promises I had made that I couldn't fix. The first promise was that I would grow up and take care of my grandmother and grandfather. I didn't get to see them again. The second, I wouldn't be like my father and be absent from my son's life. Yet again, I had broken my promise.

Days turned into weeks, and weeks turned into months, as I fought for my life. Through these long days and long nights I couldn't help but think over my life as I prayed, cried and called out to God. I went to my preliminary hearing and they read the charges out to me. They were 3 counts of armed robbery, 3 counts of aggravated assault, 3 counts of false imprisonment, burglary, and carrying a concealed weapon. My heart dropped to the ground. I couldn't believe all those charges as they bound me over to superior court.

Many days had passed, and even longer nights. Something in my heart was being pricked that I needed God. I didn't understand the thoughts, but as I thought back every time I got in trouble, I had that same tug at my heart, but I didn't know or realize at the time God was trying to get my attention. I started attending church and listening; still not understanding what was going on but I knew I needed help.

I started going through the motions and finding myself adapting to my environment. I started gambling, writing letters to my friends, going to the law library, doing all the things that people incarcerated do. I still did not believe that I was incarcerated. Where did I go wrong? Where was my father? Where was my family? I looked at every situation and person to blame. I ran into one of my homeboys from the street. He said he knew a lawyer that might have a reasonable payment plan for me. So I called my mother and made some arrangements. Yet my mother really couldn't afford a lawyer, but she tried to. He began to work on my case. I was glad that it gave me a momentary sense of hope.

One day in April, after about 2 months and some days that I was in the dorm, the officer called me out and told me to follow him upstairs to the holding cell where one of my co-defendants was also placed. I didn't understand at the time but my co-defendant told me that they questioned him about a murder, and the weapon used. I went to the detective's office and they began to ask me question after question, as I denied any involvement. The detective told me they knew my best friend killed the guy. They wanted to know was I there. They asked over and over again the same question. They held me there for a couple of hours and let me go back to my dorm. I went back in there, heart pounding. I called my mother first, and then called my lawyer and explained that they were questioning me about a murder.

I was scared because now I'm being questioned about a murder charge. How did they found out about the murder? I already had 11 felonies. I couldn't even imagine being part of a murder charge. The detectives told me that they had the shooter but they didn't know for sure if I was involved. Of course I lied to the detective, not knowing someone had already said I was involved. My heart was pounding as my life seem to be falling away from the world that I knew. They continued to question me and tried to intimidate me into confessing that I was part of this murder. They brought up the fact that the jacket I had on was reported in the murder. After a few hours they sent me back to my cell. I was in disbelief that I was involved in all this craziness. My world seemed to be getting smaller and smaller.

I tried to call out to a few friends. Some would ask what I was doing up there. My friends that I embraced as a family were talking to me like I had violated our family trust. They were not answering the phone, and when they did they were saying I needed to stop telling and running my mouth. I told them that I had not said anything. I stopped calling.

On April 22nd, my heartache became even worse than I had imagined as the officer called me back to the door. They walked me back upstairs where I met the two detectives. They handcuffed me and read me my rights, as they were charging me with murder and felony murder. That walk from the annex to the main jail was a long slow walk. My life once again passed before my eyes, and I was asking myself how in the hell did I get myself in this mess. They took me over and booked me in for murder and felony murder.

I cried because I couldn't understand how I was being charged with murder and felony murder and I hadn't murdered anyone. I was present, but I wasn't even close to the door when all this went down. I cried the whole time I was being booked in because I couldn't believe this was happening to me. It was about 2 or 3 AM when they took me to the living quarters I had to be in now. They were taking me to the East Side (E2); Thunder Dorm. I have to admit, I was terrified. I didn't know what to expect, I just knew the stories and the rumors. When they brought me to the dorm, it was dark and the doors slid open. As the door closed I was standing in dismay and staring into the dorm, seeing nothing but bunk beds with sheets wrapped around the bed where you couldn't see into the bottom bunk. Suddenly to my left a guy came out of the first bottom bunk. When he came out and stood up he resembled what I heard about guys in prison. He was wearing a do-rag and was muscular. My eyes got wide as he directed me to the bunk. I was somewhat scared as I hurried my way to my bunk. I jumped up on the bunk with swiftness. I lay there wide-eyed and thinking about all that was going on in my life. The next couple hours seemed like days. It was about 6:30 AM when breakfast was being served. Suddenly I started seeing people come out of their bunks. I was amazed. Guys were looking like something out of a movie, at least that's what I was thinking. I was just confused of all the different types of people that I saw.

I was stressed, and later that morning I had to call my mother and lawyer and tell them they charged me with murder. Through all this, all I could think about was my son.

The next several months were stressful as my inexperienced lawyer fought for my life. I got kind of used to my living quarters, as I began to meet different people, plus I was also seeing a lot of people from the street that I knew. I was still in amazement that they dropped the charges on the person who killed the person and charged me. I continued to lie and tried to stay true to the code of not snitching, not expecting the fact that I was by myself on this matter. I'll never forget my mother saying, "Do you think your so-called friends care anything about you? If they did, they wouldn't have allowed this to happen to you."

A few months passed by as I got comfortable where I was and I started adapting to the chain-gang life. I started gambling and learning how to be creative with cooking food, etc. My three outlets were basketball, masturbating, and gambling when I wanted to relieve stress. That's all that a person could do in jail.

I was there about 4 months when I got into my first fight. I injured myself on the basketball court so they wouldn't let me out on the rec yard. I stayed in the dorm. It was me and two other guys. One was the house man, the big guy, I told you about earlier. I was watching TV while everyone was gone to the rec yard. I was watching Little House on the Prairie. The house man is a person who is kind of over the dorm. His duty was to make sure we have supplies to clean up, and made sure we all had our food trays. Well for some, that meant kind of being a bully. The house man was what you think a prisoner is supposed to look like. He was built, very muscular and had an attitude. He first asked if he can check something out while it was on commercial. When I thought the commercial was over I told him I wanted to go back to the show I was watching. He told me no. We went back and forth then I told him he could have the TV. I was hoping that was over, but cursing only followed. I did all I could do to avoid him, but he kept walking towards me.

Suddenly he punched me in my face and I dropped to one knee. I kind of blanked out for split second. His next two punches dropped me to my other knee. When I stood up the last time I went into a rage and began to throw punches into his face, driving him back to the wall. He hit the wall and tried to grab me. I surely thought I was gone because I was about 168 pounds and he was about 210 pounds, nothing but muscle. But I was able to pick him up and slam him on the ground, and drew back to hit him. But I got up and backed up. He jumped up in a rage. At that moment, a guy that was still in the dorm got up and grabbed me and told me to let it go. But he wanted to keep fighting. I told him I wasn't holding back anymore. The more I looked at him the more I got mad and wanted to fight but the rage and the fight eventually was over. It was over by that time the guys were coming back to the dorm. I went and sat on my bunk and started to cry because I couldn't believe I was in jail fighting over a TV. All the guys ran to my bunk and were asking questions about the fight, ready to go jump on the guy. I told them to just let it go. He did eventually apologize.

The next several months were confusing because I was going back and forth to court. The lawyer my mother hired really started having compassion for me, yet he never defended a murder case. Over the next several months, I plead out for the armed robberies and aggravated assault and the other charges, leaving the murder charge. I plead out to 10 years for the armed robberies, aggravated assaults, false imprisonments, burglary, and firearms by a convicted felon. It really hurt to sign my name on those lines to take that time. I'll never forget turning around and seeing my mom cry. The look of embarrassment and disappointment on my mom's face was the worst moment for me that day. I could have done the time but to crush my mom's heart was punishment in and of itself.

The DA was trying to get the judge to give me a 20-year sentence but the judge wasn't going for it. The judge told me he believed I got with the wrong crowd and should do my time and become a better person. In the court room he was a comforting voice of hope. I went back to my cell with my head hanging low. A lot of the brothers were encouraging me to keep my head up.

Time went by and due to the lack of money to get an experienced lawyer, I had to do something that really put a dagger in my heart. I had to plea out to a manslaughter charge. I would have never thought I would be locked up for murder, especially when I didn't do it. I received an 18-year sentence for manslaughter running concurrently with the 10 years. I sat on my bed and wondered; was it a blessing or complete insanity to even think it was a blessing to take this 18-years. The fact I didn't get a life sentence, I guess, made it was a blessing.

On December 8, 1993 at 2:30AM, they came and woke me up and said pack your belongings, you are getting shipped to Lee Arrendale State Prison (LASP in Alto, GA). For a moment, I was excited. I thought I had escaped the infamous Alto until one of my cellmates said that is Alto. Alto was known as the second worst prison behind the

Georgia State Prison in Reidsville, but the worst for young men from the ages of 18 and 25. Alto had a history of violence and assault, both physical and sexual. Even though I know I could handle myself, there was a moment of fear not knowing what to expect and what I had to do to survive. Yet I couldn't show any fear. Fear in prison puts a target on your back. I was packing up and my cellmate said to me, "Although you and your bust partner (co-defendant) aren't seeing eye-to-eye, you are going to need friends down the road." I must say it was one of the weirdest statements, but a statement that taught me a valuable lesson in forgiveness. That was some of the best advice I'd heard in a while. When the officers brought me to the bus, one of my co-defendants, the one that I felt betrayed by, was boarding the bus as well. I had two types of feelings, one of hate and one of the joy, to see a familiar face. We boarded that bus that night and we were heading to Alto.

You can't even imagine the thoughts that went through my mind as I was riding that bus handcuffed and shackled down, heading to a place that I never thought I would see, a prison yard. As we begin to ride up North Georgia and pulled up to Lee Arrendale State Prison, aka Alto, I could only imagine in my mind what to expect. The bus pulled inside the prison gate. We were instructed to get off the bus handcuffed and shackled down and walk to intake. You see, some of the prisoners, who were already incarcerated, were looking at us like we were fresh meat as we made that walk.

The first of many days as we stood in intake, and it was a weird feeling as we listened to the yelling and screaming of officers all day. There were inmates walking in and out trying to see who the new faces were and then the humiliation of taking showers in front of a bunch of men while they shaved all my hair off and sprayed us down with lice spray. Then took us to our dorm which is called Diagnostics.

The first six weeks of being at Alto were some very trying times. The first thing that made me feel uncomfortable was the fact that I had undergo a physical exam. The doctor, who was infamous at Alto, did the prostate check, was Dr. Goldfinger. Well, that is what the inmates called him.

I'll never forget that I went through the prostate check and I went upstairs and told my mom that the doctor just gave me a prostate check and how embarrassed I was. At the age of 19, I didn't realize how important a prostate check was, but the fact that another man used his finger to check me was one of the worst moments, and funny moments, at Diagnostics, especially the look on everyone's faces when they came out of the room angry and crying. When we got down to Alto in December of 1993, it was extremely cold. It was about 30 degrees and all they gave you were a sweater and a jacket, with no skully cap. You can only imagine how harsh the climates were and they would have us on mandatory "rec call" outside in the yard. Those moments made me hate prison life, and yet it was just the beginning.

Three times a day we went to "chow call" or other words, to eat breakfast, lunch, and dinner. Honestly, being a new inmate, I hated crossing the yard because of the inmates in the other dorm, which was called B-unit, or the old annex. This is where all the level 4 and 5 guys were held. They would all be standing at the windows and looking at who they were going to try to either assault, or even worse. They used to be hollering out the window, talking about how they were going to rape us or take our personal items. I hated those moments, but it made me understand where the bad choices get you.

One day as I was walking through the kitchen line getting my food, a guy looked out the door and said I'm going to get you pretty boy when you get across the yard. I just looked and walked to my seat and it just kept ringing in my mind what that guy said. When I got back to my dorm, I called my mom and told her this place was crazy, and that I wanted to say I loved her. I also told her if these guys try to get me the way I hear other guys get raped, I am never coming home because I will kill someone. I could hear my mom crying, but she understood that it was survival.

I never knew that having good hair and being called pretty boy would be a blessing and a curse. In high school, I took it as a badge of honor because women like men with good hair. In prison, it became a burden because now you have men lusting over you. Yet I knew I had to stand strong because in this place, low self-esteem, self-pity, and not being alert can lead you into some dark places. I was determined not to be a statistic in any fashion.

The next several weeks in Diagnostics were emotional for all the guys because it was Christmas. This was the first Christmas away from my family. I met several people in Diagnostics that I got real cool with, and it was very comforting to meet people in the same mind frame. We did the best we could to try to get through the depression of being locked up away from our families. It was amazing to lie on my bunk looking down skid row watching all of the 96 guys in the dorm quiet. You hear some crying, guys talking about street life, girls, money they made, and cars they drove. The most interesting conversations were all the new stories that we were hearing about which dorms were the worst. I must say, for the most of us, there were certain dorms we just didn't want to go in.

The stories of the old annex, or B Unit to some, were something out of a horror movie. All you heard were stories of fighting, stabbings, rapes, stealing, and so on about that place. The majority were hoping to go to other units or better dorms, but either way you were still going to have to be somewhat of a stand-up guy.

While I lay in my bed, I always wondered what was going to take place. How was I going to do my time? How much time was I going to do? When would I get out? When I went to classification, I gave my agenda to the panel of administrative personnel of what I desired to do while incarcerated. I told them that I wanted to get my GED, I wanted to attend college, and I wanted to take up a couple of trades to better myself. The comment that came out of the head counselor's mouth was devastating. He told me that I have enough time to do all of that but for right now we're putting you in the kitchen. All I could do was be quiet and look down as I exited the room. I was disappointed and very angry, yet what could I do but accept it as part of prison life.

The day came when they told us to get packed up. We were heading across the yard. There were about 10 of us, with belongings packed, heading across the yard to our new dorms.

Honestly, most of us had some fear and didn't know what to expect depending on what dorm we would be put in. We didn't want to go to the 3rd floor. Dorm 13 at the time was mostly down South guys, so that wasn't good for guys from the Metro Atlanta area. Dorm 14 was mostly guys from the Metro Atlanta area, so it wasn't good for the South Georgia area. Dorm 12 was kind of laid back from what we heard. The second floor was dorm 9 through 11. Dorm 9 was the kitchen dorm. Dorm 10 was a mixture of guys from everywhere. Dorm 11 was called the rape dorm.

But, it didn't matter either way you had to be a stand-up guy, or know some people which ever dorm you got assigned to. Most guys didn't want to go to the 3rd floor or Dorm 11. I remember the look on a lot of the guys' faces as they were assigned to third floor or Dorm 11. The look was of fear, uncertainty, and disgust.

They told me to go to 2nd floor, Dorm 9. I will be assigned to first shift kitchen. It was a sigh of relief, but even though I was going to Dorm 9 there was still uncertainty because there were always inmates in every dorm that were always going to steal, try to run game, or try guys up sexually. There really was no escape from it. I went into the dorm and put my stuff on my bed, sat down, and just looked around to examine every person. The one good thing was my co-defendant came in the dorm with me, so it was a familiar face that I could trust. We talked, and both of us, I believed, were still in dismay because we were in prison. I slowly put my stuff in my box and made up my bed. A couple of hours passed by and someone said, Omar, someone wants you at the bars. I went toward the bars and it was another familiar face. It was a guy I went to high school with who had been locked up for a couple of years already for armed robbery. It was good to see old friends. We talked for a few minutes at the bars, we shook hands and he called a guy's name out that was in the dorm with me named Bob. He told Bob I was his homeboy and to make sure I am good. Bob said for sure and my high school homie walked off back to his dorm.

The day went on by as we went to Chow Hall then returned to the dorm. I used the telephone and called my family and a few friends as the night approached. I sat on my bunk and laid down before 11 PM bedtime, which is when everyone had to be in their bunks. A lot of guys were still up watching "Yo, MTV Raps" videos. A lot of the guys were still up gambling, writing and sneaking around trying to watch the girls on the videos. I sat up watching the guys that were lurking around until everyone fell asleep. It was the same routine every day. It was a madhouse for real. Every day, it seemed like a war zone on the 3rd floor as you heard the officers' radios: "1010, Dorm 13." "1010, Dorm 14." Even sometimes you heard it on the 2nd floor. "1010, Dorm 10". "1010 was the officer speak for a fight breaking out. Almost once a week you would see a guy getting raped, or "tried up" as we called, it in Dorm 11, the rape dorm. New guys were always signing P.C. or protected custody to get out that dorm.

My days as a new jack weren't easy either even though I knew a lot of guys from the street. The first couple of months, guys were always sending threats or passing by the dorm blinking their eye or saying something crazy, like "We hope you come to our dorm, we going to get you." It really bothered me that men were looking at other men like women.

It was almost humorous as I had to make a joke about it. I said to myself, dang these guys say stuff the girls used to say to me when I was in school. Only difference is these were men with evil motives. I was very alert on where I would go and who I would befriend. You couldn't trust anyone. People would set you up to get your personal items stolen out of your locker. They would get you jumped or beat up, but the worst was setting you up to get raped. It was crazy as I just tried to mind my business, keep to myself and keep my circle small. I learned very early that if you're going to get through here successfully, I would have to hear and don't hear, as long as they don't get in your face or touch you physically. But if I fight every time someone says something, I will be fighting every day, all day.

Yet, I was determined to learn how to fight. These guys were a lot bigger than me. Everyone wanted to be the best fighter, it seemed like. They had what was called the Alto shuffle, which most guys wanted to do. You always saw guys slap boxing trying to show they hand skills. Some of it was just a bluff to see if you will fight and some really knew how to fight but it was fun to learn and to watch.

I was assigned to the kitchen detail morning shift. I hated the kitchen. They had me on pots and pans for the first couple of months. We washed hundreds of pots and pans every day. It was also sickening to see guys masturbate off the female employees, and even other guys in the kitchen area. I realized prison can make you sick in the mind. This became a norm in which this was what Alto had a bad reputation for. I eventually worked my way to the serving line which was a relief from washing pans.

Six or seven months had passed by and the prison had finished their new building which was called the new B Building. There were 3 new buildings, E Building, F Building and G Building. They were condemning the old annex and sent us to the new building, which held 96 people to a dorm, 2 man cells.

But, even though I had been their several months the threat that I was going to get raped was always there. I learned to ignore a lot of the conversations and I stayed out of trouble as we moved to a new dorm. I was working in the new facility and me being the social person I am, the staff recognized I wasn't a troublemaker. I was asked what I wanted to do. I said I wanted a trade and get a GED. The staff put in for me to get moved from the kitchen to trade school. It took about a month or so for that process to go through, but before I got moved I got a visit from one of the chaplains who came to my room. I got kind of scared because normally when you got a visit from a chaplain to your room it meant something was wrong. There was even a nickname given to the chaplain because he only came when there was death in your family. They called him the Grim Reaper. So when I saw him, I kind of got scared when he opened my door and asked for me.

I jumped off my bunk and asked, "What's up, what you want?"

He kind of cracked a smile and said, "Calm down it's nothing bad, it's actually good. I notice you attend church on a consistent basis and you meet the requirements of joining the choir. I also noticed you have been consistently going to bible study. I'm here to ask would you like to join the choir?"

I looked at him and said, "Let me think about it." He said to write him a note with an answer and send it to his office. He left and I was thinking to myself that I'm still kind of ashamed of my faith because I really didn't want anyone to think I was some religious fanatic, or soft for being a church-goer. I didn't want to tell him that I hid my Bible under my shirt because I didn't want to seem weak to the other inmates. I would later learn differently, that it wasn't a sign of weakness but a sign of strength. So I waited before I gave him an answer. It was the first Sunday of the month and on that day an all-black church used to come have worship service. That service always drew a lot of the guys out for church service. Well, a lot of us didn't really go for the service but a glimpse of all the women that came. So I attended Sunday service and I saw some very beautiful women. There was one girl that took notice of me because I sat on the front row. While everyone's' heads were bowed praying, I peeped my eyes open to get a glimpse of the girls.

When I looked up we caught each other's eyes and she asked me my name. Of course, I had to read her lips. I said, Omar, and she smiled. Well, of course, other guys saw that she was asking my name. That moment made me want to get in the prison choir. The guys in the choir got to be closer to the guests, and of course I wanted to be closer.

That upcoming week I sent a letter to the chaplain to be a part of the choir and was accepted to join. Which of course I had a motive. My motive was getting my information to the young lady with hopes of gaining a pen pal. Even though I had a motive for joining the choir, I can truly say it was one of the best choices I made while I was in prison. This was the start of a journey that I never imagined. Shortly after I was accepted in the choir, the young lady that attended stopped coming. I was surely disappointed, but joining the choir helped to mature my faith as a Christian. I began to pray more, I started separating myself from a lot of negative behaviors, began to speak and lead worship service, bible studies, lead in songs, and so on. The most important part was being surrounded by like-minded people. A lot of the guys that were incarcerated began to recognize my change and respected me for it. Staff began to recognize it as well. The amazing part was a lot of the correctional officers took a liking to me and began to give me a lot of responsibility because they started trusting me.

The most amazing part was a lot of the officers that I didn't like, ended up being my allies. That didn't happen overnight; I used to pray to God let me not hate these individuals. I truly hated some of them because of the way they treated us. I watched officers curse inmates out, slap inmates, beat them up, everything you can imagine. I'm not saying that we didn't sometimes provoke a situation, but we also didn't deserve to be mistreated.

The next several years passed as I grew in age and wisdom, yet I still lacked maturity in the sense that I still struggled with trying to flirt with the female officers with the hopes of maybe having one to write me or flirt with me. It was most guys' dream and fantasy to hopefully get that opportunity. Yet because I had changed a lot and built up a lot of trust with the staff, I never wanted to get caught trying to do anything to jeopardize my trust with the staff.

I had made significant change in my life but it never ceased to amaze me that there were always strange things going on. Whether it was fights, someone getting stuck by a shank, getting their heads busted with a lock or dust mop, getting raped, or even a guy I know that got killed or the couple that died from illness. My faith had gotten stronger, but I was still disappointed that the parole panel's first response to me was they wanted me to do 13 ½ years of 18. There never was a day that I didn't hope I would go home sooner as the years kept passing by.

The year 1999 was one of the worst years for me especially when they allowed my co-defendant to go home. I was devastated, depressed, and stressed out that I didn't go home. I had been locked up almost seven years at that time. I was labeled what you would call a model inmate. I had the responsibility as a chaplain's aid, a mentor for the juveniles, and a speaker for the Scared Straight program that they had at the prison for schools that visited. Even though I had a lot of good reports and a lot of people admired my growth, leadership, and stand in my belief, there always that small crowd of people that didn't like me, lied on me, didn't trust me and loved spreading rumors. Those are the ones that really made me think about life because I couldn't understand why people never wanted to see people do well. The one thing I hated most was for a person to lie. People felt like I was too close to the officers and that I could be snitching. Some of the guys started rumors that I got raped, or even worse. But I had to understand where I was and what type of individuals I was around, and then it made sense. This was all a part of the process that I had to endure. Yet there were times where I wanted to just give up doing what had become natural, and that's to do right. I still got very depressed around holidays, birthdays, and so on. It was simple, I just wanted to go home!

The year 2000 rolled around and God opened another door. My security got dropped from medium security to minimum security. That made me eligible to go on an outside detail. I was told that I would never be able to go outside the gate with all of the charges I had and honestly, I believed it as well. Yet, God proved my doubts wrong. The first detail was working at the city of Demorest, GA at Piedmont College. I had a great time and I enjoyed every day I worked outside. To see the free world and people living their everyday lives gave me hope of a brighter day. One day when I got ready to go out for detail, the officer informed me they changed the policy and I wouldn't be going anymore. I was really disappointed. The detail officer was too. He tried to get me back on his detail. We later found out that some of the officials didn't really care for me, so that was the only excuse they could come up with even though other people were still going out despite the so called "policy change".

I was devastated, but I just dealt with it. I was assigned to be a visitation room orderly. This wasn't a bad detail, and besides the hard labor, I kind of enjoyed it. This also was the place where we did the Scared Straight with the schools that came to tour our prison. I became the lead speaker which I really enjoyed. I was on this detail for a couple of months.

One day, I was getting ready to go to yard call. It was a very nice day and I really wanted to play basketball. I went down to put up all the chairs as we do after every visitation. I went back up to the officer to report that we were done and that we wanted to go play basketball. But, for some reason she was taking her time. I got real impatient and she and I had a few words. Nothing I thought was too serious, but later that day would tell a different story. I got back to the dorm and we went out and played basketball and had a great time.

We came back to the dorm and I got into the shower to end the rest of my day and get prepared for tomorrow as I do every day. While I was taking a shower, I heard my name being called. I said I was in the shower. Five minutes passed and the officer came to the shower door and said you need to report down stairs. I said ok as I got out the shower to put on my clothes. The officer called my name again and said hurry up. I threw on my clothes thinking they needed me to do something on my detail. When I walked down the stairs the sergeant said put your hands behind your back. I asked, for what? He said just do as I tell you to do. So I put my hands behind my back as he put handcuffs on me and walked me out of the building to the lieutenant's office. I looked at the lieutenant and asked him what's going on. He said the major told him to send me to the block because I was under investigation.

I asked for what, of course. He said he couldn't tell me and that they will see me tomorrow when they get into work. They walked me to solitary confinement, which was also called Special Management Unit (SMU). I was devastated because it had been almost 8 years at Alto and I had never been to the hole. I walked into SMU, and they took me to my holding cell. A lot of the inmates in the hole were calling my name, asking what I was doing there. All I could say was. I don't know.

They put me in my holding cell and for the next hour I just sat there trying to figure out what did I do? The inmate next to me was a young man that I had the opportunity to talk with, we talked mostly all night about life, religion, family, and so on.

He later told me that he really enjoyed our conversation and that it was encouraging. We both said our goodnights. Before I closed my eyes, I thanked God that even though I'm in the hole, I had an opportunity to encourage someone. The next morning, they made the call that it was inspection time. The warden and his staff normally came through to check each dorm every morning for cleanliness. When they got to my room the warden looked and was stunned and asked what are you doing in here? I said, sir I don't know. The major said that he was going to talk to me later after inspection. It was about 3 or 4 hours later when the major decided to come get me. But before he came and got me several staff members came to check on me and asked what I was locked down for, and of course I said I don't know. Finally, an officer came and got me to take me to the major's office. He handcuffed me and walked me across the yard. While on my way, a lot of my friends were like, "Omar, what they lock you up for?"

All I could say was, "I don't know."

When I walked into the major's office and sat down, he said, "You know why we locked you down?"

I said, "No sir."

He said, "The officer said you were acting all weird and suspicious. So they went down and checked the visitation room and found cookies and snacks in the vending machine. We had inmates in the past on this detail that got caught with drugs and we were wondering if you were getting anything from the vending man."

I looked at him said, "Sir, I don't even touch the machines. I just sweep, mop, and buff floors. I didn't know there was anything in the vending machine slot. Rewind the tapes. I never even went close to the machines." The major said he believed me, but he had to do this to make sure I wasn't getting anything illegal through the vending machine worker. He told me I would be back in the dorm today.

When I got back to the dorm I was disappointed for the fact I got sent to the hole for some cookies. I actually had to laugh to myself. I've been at one of the worst prisons in Georgia and never went to the hole for anything like stealing or fighting but this one time was for cookies. I bowed my head to pray and I credited being here to God because I was able to lift someone's spirit even when mine was down. My next-door cellmate in the hole was kind of sad that I was going back to my dorm, but he constantly thanked me for encouraging him through this difficult time.

I went back to my dorm about 3:00pm that evening and started back on my detail the next day. To my amazement, a lot of the staff walked by and said they were concerned about me. One went on to even say a lot of people were on my side and pulling for me. I could only smile, and tell them they don't know how much that meant to me.

A month or so went by and I was awakened in the middle of the night by an officer with words I didn't really want to hear. She said, "Pack it up Omar, you're getting transferred." I took a deep breath as I sat on side my bed for a few minutes just wondering where was I being transferred to. I've been here 8 1/2years. I was comfortable, and I was only an hour and 45 minutes away from my family. I really didn't want to go. I established myself as a model inmate, yet my journey at the legendary Alto was over.

I didn't know what to think, but for a moment as I packed my belongings I thought about everything that I had been through and all I had accomplished. I must say, I surely matured as a Christian. I met a lot of good brothers, got my GED, and completed a lot of self-help programs. I was a chaplain's aid and I sang in the choir for about 5 years. I was a speaker for the Scared Straight Program and a mentor for the juveniles. I was well-respected amongst the staff here, and now I had to start all over again not knowing what to expect or where I was going. There were some very discouraging moments, but there were a lot of fun and joyful moments. A few fights, a lot of arguments, some lies were told about me, a lot of hate, but despite it all, I made it through. I didn't get caught in the wave of negativity or violence. I didn't mess with men sexually, I didn't get raped, and I didn't get shanked. A few minor issues, but for the most part, I beat the odds because I was determined to be different.

There was one thing that bothered me as I finished packing my belongings, where were they going to transfer me? There are over 30 state prisons in Georgia and they can transfer you to any one of them at any time. Would I be close enough for my mother to come visit? Or would I be sent far away? I wrote my number down on a piece of paper and told my roommate to call my mother the next morning and let her know I got transferred. I finished packing and the officer took me to intake. We were handcuffed and put on the bus. It was a 4 hour ride to Jackson State Prison where all the transfers are finalized and you are told where your destination prison will be. That bus ride was so uncomfortable and long. There was absolute silence on the bus as everyone was trying to figure out where they were going. It was about 4:30 AM when we pulled arrived at Jackson State Prison. They have everyone standing out on the pavement with their belongings. They call out what bus to get on, one by one. They called my name and my EF number #316767. They said you will be going to the Burruss Correctional Training Center bus. Actually it was just a van. Only about 3 guys got on this bus and we drove off handcuffed, but not shackled this time. We drove for about 30 min until we reached Forsythe, GA in Monroe County. I was surprised at how close we were to the prison.

Burruss Correctional Training Center, as I found out, was the training center for public service workers to take classes, update their training, and so on. I had heard about this facility, and that it was said to be a good facility. It was a medium security camp, one man cells that had air conditioning. Rumor was it took an act of congress to get placed at Burruss.

This surely was an upgrade from Alto. There were only about 500 inmates at this facility compared to 1500 at Alto. Plus, this was a privileged prison because of the public service employees who came to train at the facility. I was somewhat sad until I found out that I was less than an hour away from my mother. I got real excited to know that my mother didn't have to drive that far to see me.

This new journey surely had to be better, at least I hoped, since Alto wasn't as bad as I had feared. I had hopes that things were looking up. The officer said if you arrived here you are probably getting ready to get paroled. I got super excited being here. The first week there, I ran into several guys that I knew from Alto. It was good seeing familiar faces. They told me the "do's and the don'ts". I took heed to what they were saying to make the new transition as best it could be.

The next week I got classified to see where they were going to place me at Burruss. Several other guys and I were getting classified that day, including the guys that came in the same day I did. I was called into a room where I sat in front of the Classification Committee. They told me that they couldn't believe that I came from Alto and had not had a disciplinary report in 7 years.

They were in awe, and asked me a lot of questions about the things I did there and how I had such a clean institutional record. They said most guys that come from Alto have a long disciplinary record, but I was the first that they've seen with such an impeccable record. I explained all that I did and what I was involved in as far as being a chaplain aide, mentor to juveniles, speaker for the Scared Straight Program, and so on. They were impressed, and for about 30 minutes they went back and forth on what detail I should be on. One said, technically because of all your charges, even though you have minimum security, we are not supposed to let you out of the gate. They couldn't come to an agreement while I was in the room and they had some more guys waiting to be classified, so they asked me to wait outside. Another guy went in for about 15 minutes and came out. He asked, "Who is Omar?"

I said, "Me, why what's up?"

He said, "They were supposed to be talking about me, but they're in there talking about you. Saying you must be a miracle child or something to survive through that place without getting a lot of DR's (Disciplinary Reports)." I kind of smiled knowing that they were having a positive discussion about me.

They called me back in the room, and to my amazement they were still discussing whether to let me out of the gate or put me on a detail inside of the gate. I explained that I was approved at Alto to go out of the gate until they changed the policy. The sergeant said they needed to put me outside the gate since I had such a clean record and positive attitude. She said they needed to let me prove myself. They decided to put me at the front gate where I would see everyone that comes in from the warden and all his staff. Sometimes you would see special guests like the Commissioner of the Department of Corrections. This was to prove how responsible of an inmate I was. I had one more question before I left, I asked why I was transferred from Alto? They said that you were too familiar with staff, meaning too many staff members knew you and you knew them. They said, have a good day Mr. Howard, we are trusting you to shine and do a great job. I said, I will.

The front gate detail was surely a challenge. The officer in charge wasn't a pleasant lady, and honestly, after a couple of weeks I hated that detail. I had to be out in the elements all day for 8 hours straight. I had to cut grass, plant flowers, pick up leaves, walk the parking lot and pick up trash. The officer never wanted to see me sitting down for a minute. I had learn to pray harder and harder every day if I wanted to stay on outside detail, because I knew I could mess up. I was on this detail for about 8 months and hated it but kept those thoughts to only myself. I finally got to a place where I could request a detail change and I was excited that I got approved for a change, thinking I was going to go to a better detail. I learned quickly to watch what I ask for. I got my detail changed to what we call the cone course. It's where the police force did driver training. This detail was the worst, it was the front gate detail intensified 5 times. I was miserable, but I knew that I had to stay focused if I was to make it through this moment in my life.

While I complained about the detail there were a few things that kept me grounded. I joined the choir at Burruss, which kept me very active. I also became a chaplain aid as well. It was amazing because, for a short period of time, we didn't have a chaplain, so we had to conduct services and make sure things were in order. Having this task surely made me understand the role of a chaplain better. We held service every week as well as other activities for the staff. What was amazing, after being at Burruss for about 8 months to a year, I was receiving letters from fellow inmates from Alto who were either still at Alto or transferred to another prison. It brought tears and joy to me to know that a lot of guys looked up to me and reached out on their own to tell me that they had gotten saved and I set a good example for them to give their life to Christ. I was so humbled to receive these letters because guys recognized my struggles and my walk in Christ. I was humbled even more when several volunteers reached out through mail and wrote how much they missed my presence and that it wasn't the same without me. It made me cry because I didn't realize the impact I was having on others. But it felt good to know people cared. It made me want to be better and to keep pushing forward to be my best.

I was finally transferred off the cone detail. They assigned me to the big kitchen where I was able to learn different cooking skills. I really enjoyed being in the kitchen and cooking for the staff as well as the inmates back at the prison. I stayed in the kitchen over a year and built a lot of good relationships with the staff, but I could never forget that I was still in prison and that I still had to deal with issues. One day, a brother and I had some harsh words that lead to him pushing me. I didn't want to fight right then, but I made sure he knew we were going to fight when we got back to the dorm. That whole day I was mad, didn't want to talk to anyone, I just wanted to fight. One of the staff members even came and said, "It's not worth it. Don't get in any trouble. You are trying to accomplish something in your life and you are trying to get transferred to the halfway house." But I was so mad, all I could do was think about fighting. I was putting everything on the line knowing you couldn't go to the halfway house if you got a disciplinary record.

We got on the bus and returned to the prison. Everyone on the bus was quiet because they knew there was tension in the air. I got back to the dorm, went to my room, took off my shirt and walked back down stairs. I told the guy come on in the room and let's resolve this issue. He was bigger than me, but it didn't matter, we had to resolve this issue. There were a couple of punches thrown and we grabbed each other. Other inmates ran in the room and pulled us apart and said it's over. I didn't realize he was bleeding until I got back to my room and had blood all over my hands.

When I locked the door behind me, I sat on my bed and was thinking that I just messed up my opportunity to go to the halfway house. Surely, he was going to say something about us fighting. I sat in the same spot for a couple of hours just thinking of how stupid I was for acting out. Suddenly, I got a knock on my door. My eyes got big. It was the guy that I was fighting with. He said, "Let me in Omar." I grabbed my boots, put them back on and was ready for another fight. He said, "The fight is over, you got the best of me. But don't think I'm going to stop talking because you know how I am, let's go grab a bite to eat from the chow hall." I was amazed at his response, he didn't say anything even though the word got around we had a fight. We became good friends after the altercation. He got to go home shortly after that. I was down there for several more months. A lot happened in the last months that I was at Burruss. My mother's health wasn't all that good and I started to stress-out because I had been locked up for 11 ½ years now. I didn't know if I was going to get out anytime soon or not.

One day, while rehearsing with one of the choir members, we started having a discussion about prison, parole, family, everything. He told me there was a guy by the name of Mark next door, whose sister has an organization that is trying to help people in prison. That I should to talk to him to see if his sister, who is the founder, will help you. I thought about it because over the years I've written, talked to, begged and pleaded with people to help. The same story all the time, they lead me to believe that they were going to do something to try to help, but end up disappearing without a trace and leaving me hopeless and in doubt. I lost faith in people and asking them for help. I decided to take a chance and reach out to Mark and ask about his sister's organization. That night, I went to the door and asked for Mark, not knowing who he was or what he looked like. When he came to the door he looked like this mean, hairy face white guy that did not like black people, at least that was my first impression. I started to talk with him and we stayed at the door talking for about an hour and I must say what I thought of him was the total opposite. Actually he was a very kind guy and he listened to me spill my life story. He said, "You seem to be a nice guy and people speak highly about you. I'm going to give you my sister's number and I'm going to call her and let her know you will call her tonight. Just be honest with her." I must say for some reason I was very excited as I went back to my room anticipating calling her and introducing myself. I finally got to the phone to call her and she answered. I introduced myself and she introduced herself as Andrea and told me a little bit about herself and her organization, HeartBound Ministries. I was excited about meeting her and she actually took a liking to me and offered to help me.

My mother was having medical issues and couldn't drive. Andrea and her mother offered to go pick up my mom and bring her up to see me on visitation day. I was most humbled by the generosity. Over the coming months, we communicated as I shared my information with her with hoped she would be able to help convince the parole board to let me out. It was finally nice to meet someone who actually tried to help.

One night the officer came to my door and said, "Omar Howard, pack it up you getting transferred." My heart dropped to the ground, not again as I start to feel that feeling when I was transferred from Alto not knowing where I was going. My heart was pounding as I sat on side of the bed. I packed my stuff and about an hour later the officer came and got me and they took me to intake. When I got to intake it was about 40 guys in the holding room. I asked what was going on. The guys said they're doing an emergency transfer of guys because a lot of illegal drugs were found in the prison. All I could think was how did my name get tied up in this? I don't smoke nor do I get in any illegal drugs. They inventoried everyone's belongings and took us to the van for transport. I could not believe I was being transferred along with these guys for something I knew nothing about. I was stressed as they took us out to the van to go back to Jackson State Prison. When we arrived at Jackson, they ordered us off the van. They instructed guys to different transfer buses to send them to other prisons. I was the last one. The Sergeant approached me. He said, "Do you know where you going son?"

I put my head down and said, "No sir."

He said. "You are going to the Atlanta Transitional Center, you're going home soon."

I dropped my head in disbelief, because I was trying for the last year or so to get to the work release center. I was the only one out of 40 guys that night getting transferred to a transitional center. I didn't know if to scream or cry. One thing for sure, I was excited! They took the handcuffs off as I boarded the van. This was the first time since I've been incarcerated that I didn't have to wear handcuffs when I boarded a prison vehicle! That may not sound like much to a free man but it meant a lot to me! The last journey of my life as a state prisoner was December 9, 2003 as I was heading to the transitional center.

The Atlanta Transitional Center was the best place a person could be, especially to finish up your time. There were two parts of a transitional center. Long term maintenance and work release. I was assigned to long term. It was a privilege to be here, meaning you had to have a good institutional record. While being in long term maintenance, you were assigned to state details like the governor's mansion, state capitol, Georgia building authority, kitchen details around the transitional center, and Georgia State

Patrol. You could be there as long as 3 1/2 half years to your release date or max-out date.

Work release meant you were 9 months or less to paroling out. You had an opportunity to get a job and make some income. Both sides were able to wear civilian clothes. The transitional center was very structured and strict, preparing you for life in the real world. I remember riding in the van heading up 75 north. As we entered the city limits we could see the buildings starting to emerge over the horizon. The closer we got, the more excited I got knowing I was close to home.

We arrived and went through the whole process of intake as they took inventory of what we can have and not have. The officer told us all the rules and gave us a brown jumpsuit to wear for 30 days. When we finished up in intake, they assigned us to our rooms. It was about 6PM when they allowed me to make a phone call. I was so excited to call and tell my mom. I dialed the number and my mom picked up.

She sounded so sad as if I was going to tell her I got moved too far for her to come see me. Burruss was only 45 min from her before and she was wondering where her son would be now? I said, "Momma you are not going to believe this! I'm in Atlanta! Off Ponce de Leon. At the transitional house! Twenty minutes away from you!" I could hear her sounds of laughter and crying with joy. I only wished I could see her face as I told her how close I was to her and my son. I told her of all the benefits of being there. I got off the phone and talked to a few guys that I knew from prison and they told me the "do's and don'ts" until it was time to go to bed.

That night, all I could do was lay on top of my bunk and praise God for the opportunity. I laid there, looking out the window for most of the night. How beautiful the city lights looked. It had been almost 12 years since I've seen the city of Atlanta and if I do what I'm supposed to do, I could be going home in about a year. At least that was the plan.

The next 12 months were fun being able to see my mom, my sons and even some old friends made their way around to drop off clothes and money. We had the privilege to go to the grocery store, of course with police escort. I will never forget the first time walking in the grocery store to get my approved items and walking to the self-checkout. Times had really changed. I had never seen a self-checkout, and of course they had to help me, but it was cool.

I was assigned to kitchen detail because I wasn't eligible to go outside the center until I was in work release. It was cool, but with every institution I had to adjust to the system. One of the residents, as they call you in the transitional center, pulled me to the side one day and made a very powerful statement. He had seen me struggling with the rules at times. He said, "Omar this place demands change. You are going to be going home one day from here, you got to be ready." I took those wise words to heart because it was very easy to get sent back to prison if you didn't adjust yourself to the rules.

A year passed. I joined the church choir and began to make a good name for myself. I was even awarded the opportunity to be over the Chaplain library and over all the church services because we didn't have a chaplain at the time.

One day while on my detail working, the Superintendent called for me to come to his office and made a statement that blew me away. He said, "Omar, I was looking for someone to take over my library and I think I got the right man. You. I'm going to treat you like a volunteer, anything you need you get with the assistant superintendent and we will make it happen. Don't let me down. If you have any problems from anyone let me know."

I was overwhelmed by his statement because he never really gets involved in the assigning of details. The next three or four months I did just that. I oversaw the Chaplain department and all the responsibilities that came along with maintaining the chaplaincy. Along with this responsibility, came jealousy from residents and staff as most of them thought the warden was giving me too much freedom. Several months passed and the Superintendent came to me and said, "I think we found a great man that will be our next Chaplain, he will start in February." I was excited that we had finally found a person that would take that position. His name was Chaplain Nix. He was a very passionate guy and someone over the next year that inspired me to keep pushing to take my place in manhood and to stand in my calling. I really never encountered a man that was so genuine, so loving and a true man of God.

The 2005 year was exciting as Chaplain Nix brought a lot of volunteers and classes to the center. Things that surely helped me grow as an individual and not just me but everyone that Chaplain Nix came in contact with. Our choir grew strong in 2005, we had 15 members and our church services was growing in attendance.

That same year the Clayton County Juvenile Court reached out to the warden and requested me to come out to a program called Project HIP to speak to their at-risk youth who were court appointed to the program. They said a young man who got out of prison spoke highly of Omar and how positive of a person he was and what he had done while he was in prison. The warden approved for them to come to the center to interview me and asked would I consider doing this. I said gladly, I would love to come out and share my testimony. Hopefully they will learn and change their lives. It was amazing because I had been praying about this, talking about going out to the schools to talk with the kids about choices & consequences. My prayers was finally answered.

The first day I went out, the warden drove me himself. I poured my heart out to those kids that day and got a response from all of the kids and from the parents. When we left, the warden told me I did a great job. The following week they asked the warden if I could come back every month, and he said yes. They eventually brought a couple more guys in to help out with the program.

I was enjoying myself, as I was preparing to hopefully be going into work release soon. One day, as my family was leaving visitation, I whispered in my mom's ear and said, "Hey, I will be coming home soon. So we're going to surprise my son."

She said, "Ok", as she walked out the door. While I was in the control room to get my I.D., they said your counselor wants you to report to his office. I walked to his office not even recognizing there was an officer behind me.

When I got to his office he said, "I've got some good news and some bad news for you, which one you want to hear first?"

I said of course, "The bad news."

He said, "Well, the parole board did not approve of you going into the work release at this time. They denied it and set you off to do 3 ½ more years in prison. The good news is, we don't have to send you back to prison. You meet the requirements to stay here at the Atlanta Transitional Center until you come up again for parole."

I put my head down dejected and walked out of the office. I couldn't believe what I just heard. The Parole Board wanted me to do 3 ½ more years. I've already done 12 years in prison. There were a lot of thoughts going through my head. How can I go tell my mom after I just told her an hour ago that I will be coming home soon? How can I be away from my son for 3 more years? Why me God? I've done all that I was asked to do? Will I make it another 3 ½ years in here? I wasn't sure of my thoughts any more as I walked around in disbelief.

The word spread around the center quickly. The officers and other residents kept telling me to keep my head up. I was a zombie for a couple of hours.

I was standing in the hallway when the warden passed by and said, "Omar come to my office, let me talk to you." I slowly walked into his office as he closed the door. He said, "I'm aware that the parole board denied you to go into work release and possibly going home soon. I don't know why they did it because there was no explanation. I don't know how you feel, but I want to encourage you that you have a purpose here and I want you to stay here where people care about you. You have a choice and the choice is yours. Go back to prison or stay here, I prefer you stay here."

I looked up at him with tears in my eyes and said, "I'm hurt but I'm not crazy. I don't want to go back to prison."

We both smiled and he said, "Now, I'm not changing your detail. I want you to stay focused until better days come."

I got up and he shook my hand and I went to my room and laid down. My roommate said, "I'm sorry to hear about your set-off time but don't let this situation beat you down, you can rise up out this." I listened to him and cried a little then got up out of bed to go call my mom.

This was a hard call to make. I just told her earlier when she came to visit that I was coming home soon. Now I had to tell her the bad news, that they denied me and I had 3 ½ more years. When she answered the phone and I told her, she just started crying. I said, "Well mom, one good thing they are not going to send me back to prison. I just got to keep fighting through this." We said our goodbyes for the night and I hung up. The next several days were pretty hard because even though people were trying to comfort me, every time it brought back the pain knowing I was going to be there for 3 ½ more years.

I must say, the next 12 months were intense as our choir was being requested to come speak to churches and youth programs all around the state of Georgia. We were also featured in the Atlanta Journal Constitution and the news channels concerning redemption from behind the walls.

One day, we got a request to come sing at the chaplain of the Department of Corrections retirement party. The commissioner invited us after he heard us sing at an event. We performed and had a great time and the event was awesome. There was a young lady that asked to see the chaplain after the event because she enjoyed hearing the choir. Chaplain Nix set up a date for her to come visit. The day when she came to visit Chaplain Nix, she explained what she was doing and that she wanted to adopt the transitional center to help bring programs there and however else they could help. Her ministry was called HeartBound Ministry.

When she got ready to leave, the chaplain told her that he wanted to introduce her to his chaplain's aid.

As she and I began to talk, we both looked at each other and instantly realized we knew each other. It was Andrea! All we could do was smile and laugh as we hugged. It was amazing, the person that I only knew from phone conversations and the kindness that she displayed by bringing my mother to come see me was finally rewarded as we meet face to face.

The next couple of years, we had a great time working alongside Clayton County Juvenile court Project HIP program and with The Department of Corrections who were allowing us to do youth intervention. They called it "Make the right choice, choose freedom" campaign. The commissioner's vision was to encourage young people to choose a better path in life and, if they did, we could slow the rapid growth of the prison population.

Regardless of how much fun we were having, the pain of prison life still lingered and the urge to want to be free always was present in our minds. Being the face of the choir and speaking engagements brought on a lot of dislike from residents as well as staff.

In 2006, it came time for me to put in for early parole consideration. There was a good chance that I could go home in August 2007, if the parole board approved it or I would have to wait until April 2008. I wrote a letter to all the parole board members asking to be given a chance at parole. I was desperate. I was ready to go home, I was tired.

A couple of months passed by and still no word. But I stayed the course and even though I was stressed, I tried not to show it. The fact that I was able to go out and encourage others not to make the same choices I made, really kept me encouraged. One day I received some legal mail from the parole board that said, "Your file is under investigation and we will contact you by mail when the parole board makes a decision." It also said, "We recognize your institutional conduct and we encourage you to continue." It was rewarding to know they were considering me for parole, but that wasn't a guarantee especially when I've been denied before. Months went by and not a word from them. I was starting to stress again because I wanted to go home and be with my family. I've been incarcerated for 14 years on an 18 year sentence

My counselor called me to his office in February of 2007 and said, "I've got some good news. The parole board has considered giving you your date for August 2007, pending you complete the work release program." I couldn't believe that I finally got the news I've been waiting for over 14 years, the opportunity to be released. I was so excited and filled with joy. I told him I'm going to surprise my mother when she comes to visit me.

That weekend my mother visited and we talked for a few hours. When she got ready to leave, I grabbed her arm, leaned in close to hug her and kiss her on the cheek. I whispered in ear, "Mom, they approved me for work release, I come home in August." My mother bowed her head in relief, as she smiled and walked off in joy.

The same week, Andrea and Chaplain Nix were asked to come to TBN broadcasting to do a television interview about prison. I was also asked to be a part of the interview. I was excited especially when being asked how I feel. I said I'm excited that I've been given the chance to go into work release. The interview last about 30 minutes. One of the last questions was, "If you could start over, what would you be when you grow up and what you would tell the younger audience?"

I said if could start over I would be a good father. My closing statement on the television show to the younger audience was that freedom is a choice. The Host, repeated what I said and ended the interview with please choose wisely.

It seemed like everything I asked for was coming to pass. In work release, the privilege of working a real job and saving some money was rewarding. Also, the privilege to go home on 6 to 12 hour passes on your days off was the highlight of being in work release. I couldn't wait to go home for the first time since 1993 to embrace my son and my family. I started working in March 2007 for a battery company in Lithonia, Ga. The second job that I ever had and I was excited. I worked 3rd shift. The first time riding a Marta bus seemed so rewarding; heading out by myself to go to work and having consistent money on my account. Then having the opportunity to buy my son his first cell phone and keeping up the phone bill from prison. As the months went by, my excitement grew. I was very active in the choir and speaking engagements. Life seemed so beautiful, what could possibly go wrong.

In July 2007, one month before the parole board made a final decision, I got some disturbing news from them.

The strangest part was that no one understood the news. The parole board said that I couldn't parole to my mother's house because it was too close to a school. The assistant superintendent asked for the reason. The parole officer said it was because of the sexual offense charge that's my file. I told them that I didn't have a sexual offense charge and they must have me mixed up with someone else.

The parole officer said I was right, that I didn't have a sex charge but for some reason there is a red sticker on my file indicating that I fall under the sex offense law from a prior conviction. He told me he would find out why and get back to me with an explanation.

I couldn't believe what I was hearing and neither did the assistant superintendent. We were both devastated with what we just heard. Two hours passed when the parole officer called back and it was confirmed that I had to register as a sex offender. He explained that back in 1996, Georgia passed a law concerning what specific charges would be put

125

under a new bill. They were targeting people who had crimes where a minor was involved. It didn't have to be of a sexual nature, but the mere fact a certain crime was committed against a child under 17. One of my charges was false imprisonment that involved three people and a minor was one of them which qualified me to be put under the sex offense policy. They made it retroactive which made any and everyone who had these type of charges before and after 1996 fall under this law. The parole officer did not agree with it and really didn't understand it but he had to follow policy. My mother's address was not approved due to the restrictions of the law. I couldn't believe what I was hearing. The superintendent, the chaplain, Andrea and other people who were involved in my life were informed and of course, everyone was reaching out to resources to see what could be done, if anything.

All leads came back to the same conclusion, I would have to register as a sex offender. I couldn't go to my mom's house because she stayed too close to a school. The parole officer told me to look for a different place to stay and submit it so I could get home soon. That would be the only way they would release me. In my mind, all I could ask was why do I always seem to get disappointed when things seem to start going right for me? Why do I keep suffering for things I haven't done? Once again, I had to call my mother with disturbing news. What will I tell my son? That his dad isn't coming home in August?

One thing for sure was I had to look for a place to stay because I was ready to go home. The next 4 months were critical for me. Every day, when I had an opportunity in between work and coming back to the center, I looked for a place that met the criteria. The criteria was you couldn't stay within a 1000 feet of a school, park, church, playground, daycare, mall, bus stop or anywhere kids gather. That's pretty much everywhere on the planet. There are churches on every corner it seemed like in Decatur where I was moving. I had started feeling hopeless and stressed every day. My prayer every day was, "God why me? Show me what to do."

I continued my search vigorously and still came up with nothing. Then one day, a friend of the center came to me and said, "I got someone who is willing to let you rent their condo in Sandy Springs. He is part of my bible study group. I told everyone what you were dealing with and he said he is willing to help."

I was excited but had to put the location in to see if it was approved with the parole board. I was so excited that I didn't even check to see if it was within a 1000 feet of a school. We sent the info to the parole board with hopes that it would get approved. I went to work every day as usual and did everything I was supposed to do. A couple of weeks passed by with no answer at all. I called the phone number to see if a date was set and as I figured, no date was set. I started to get scared of another rejection from the parole board. It was the first week of December and I said let me make a call today to see if there has been any changes. I called the parole board number not knowing what to expect when the recorder came on and said, there has been a release date of December 10, 2007. I dropped the phone to my side as I closed my eyes in relief that the address had been approved. I was finally going home!

Dec 10, 2007 was my released day from prison. You would have thought things were going smoothly as they were supposed to that morning. I woke up and did my grooming routine, put on my clothes and went over to talk with the warden to sign all of my papers and leave, but there was problem. My landlord had not brought me my keys so I could go check into my new place. Normally after a person signs their papers they leave about 9AM. It was 10 o'clock before I reached my landlord and set up a time to meet me with the keys. The assistant superintendent was told by the warden to take me to meet my mother. Finally, I walked out of the Atlanta Transitional Center and out of prison for good.

I finally could smile with joy as I went to meet my mom and rejoice that I was finally set free.

I'll never forget meeting my mom and getting in the car with her. It was the best day since my son was born 16 years before. We rode to the condo that I was renting. I went in and gave the guy his money for the first month's rent, $900. I told them I'll be back shortly after I do a little shopping for the condo. I was so excited to finally be free. Thinking of all the things that I wanted to do was exhilarating. I went to a few department stores to pick a few items and we also went to eat and talk about life.

Several hours passed by as we were riding around thinking of things to put in my condo. I told mom I needed to call my parole officer to tell them I'll report tomorrow morning since I had 24 hours to report. I called my parole officer and told them that I would be reporting first thing in the morning. I was stopped in the middle of my sentence by the assistant chief and was told to report immediately to the office. I told him I'll be there in about 30 min. It was 3:30 PM. I said, "Mom, they want me to report to the parole office today. They probably want me to put the leg monitor on so I got to report now."

We pulled up to the office and asked my mom to just stay in the car and let me go in and get the information they need me to get and I'll be back out in a few minutes. It was about 4:15 and the office closed at 5. I sat there waiting until 4:30 when the assistant chief came and invited me to his office. He introduced himself and told me something that would rock my world. He said, "The condo that you have, you can't stay there because it's too close to a school. We made a mistake of approving that address. You shouldn't have gotten out." I was floored! He continued, "You've got to find another place to live. If not, we are sending you back to jail until you find an address that meets the requirements. You got 'til 5 PM to find a place to live."

I looked at him said, "Sir, I've been locked up 15 years! How am I gonna find a place to live in 15 minutes?"

He replied, "That's your business." I sat there in disbeliefof what I just heard. I was speechless as I asked if I could use his phone. I immediately called the transitional center and told the warden and the assistant superintendent and the chaplain. Everyone was in disbelief and shocked. They began to make calls to the parole board and to whomever else they could think of.

The superintendent even talked to the assistant chief and of course, there wasn't much that could be done. I walked outside and told my mom to come into the office so I could break the news. It really hurt me to see my mother struggle with what I was saying. We sat in the office until 5 PM. The parole officer said, "Let me say this, it's too late for me to put a warrant on you to arrest you. "I need for you to find a place to stay until tomorrow and be here by 9 AM when the office opens. Listen, I'm not telling you to  stay at your mom's house for tonight because she stays too close to a school. So find somewhere to stay until in the morning."

My mother and I got up and went to the car and drove to her house. I had to find a hotel to stay for tonight. I watched my mother almost have a nervous breakdown, crying so hard because she couldn't believe I was going through all this. I found a hotel called the Atlanta Hotel on Moreland Ave. It was not that pleasant of a place to stay, but I did as I was instructed. I cried most of the night. All I could say, "Is God why me?" This was supposed to be one of the best days of my life and yet it's been simply horrible. It started with trying to get my keys from the landlord which delayed me from leaving the transitional center early. I finally left 2 hours late because the people were just moving out my condo that day. Also, I called the landlord to tell him about the problem with the location, but he wouldn't refund it so I lost all of that money.

To top it all off, I had to find a new place to live before 5 PM the next day or I'm going back to prison! I paid for the room and went and laid down on the bed. I didn't even care that it wasn't pleasant in that hotel room. I was stressed out at that moment, without hope. I got a phone call from a friend that was aware what was going on and she insisted to come and see me at the hotel. I let her in when she arrived. I laid back across the bed as she walked over and held me. I curled up in her arms like a little baby and cried myself to sleep.

I woke up that morning not knowing what to expect as my mother pulled up to take me to the parole office. I went in and met my assigned parole officer. She seemed to be very nice but she had a job to do and that was to tell me to go look for a place to live. I started at 10 AM looking for a livable place that met the sex offender requirements. It had to be 1000 feet from schools or play grounds or anywhere kids congregate. I went online, Craigslist, newspaper, Google, and so on but not one place met the requirements. I felt the clock ticking. I started panicking when I looked at the time. It was 3 PM and the parole office closed at 5. I had to have a place to live by 4 o'clock or I was going back to jail.

My phone rang. It was Andrea from HeartBound. She said she wanted me to check out this transitional house and call them immediately and see if they will accept you. I called and the owner picked up the phone and we talked. I told what I was up against and he asked if I could get there by 3:30 for an interview. He gave me the address and I told him I'll see him shortly. I told my parole officer and went on my way to the interview to see if I qualified to come to the transitional home. I arrived and met with the owner and his wife and a representative of the transitional home.

We talked for about 30 minutes and I explained my situation to him. He understood and said that he would accept me as long as I abide by the rules. I had to pay $125 a week for room and board. So I gave him $500 for the whole month. I called my parole office and she approved the address. It was such a relief to know I wasn't going back to prison. It was about 1 hour before I would have been locked up to sit in prison until I found a place to live. I brought in my belongings as I moved into one of the rooms where I shared an apartment with 2 other residents. I was relieved, but I wasn't happy. I went from moving into a condominium to staying in a drug rehabilitation transitional home within 24 hours of me being paroled. It almost felt like I was back in prison but with a few more privileges.

I was happy that I was out of prison and that I was working making money. I worked 3rd shift so I worked through the night and came back to the room to sleep through most of the day, unless I had some errands to run. I still had to call and report every time I left the apartment because I was on a strict curfew. I had a leg monitor and it called at certain times of the night or day depending on what I was doing.

A few days passed and I was starting to feel a little better that I was out of prison. It was Friday and I just got off work that morning and made it home about 11 AM. When I got in my room and settled down, I got a phone call from my parole officer. She asked how my day went and how was work coming along. I was telling her I'm just glad to be free and I'm doing well. Then she said, "Omar, I need for you to do something this weekend for me."

I said, "Ok what do I need to do?"

She said, "My Assistant Chief came to me and said that the park near the center is about 15 feet short of the 1000 feet rule. I need to find a place to live by Monday or they're going to locking you up." My chin fell to my chest in disbelief. I couldn't believe this was happening to me. She said, "I'm sorry this is happening to you, I don't understand or agree with the policy, but I have to enforce it. Please beat the pavement and find a place to live."

How can this be happening to me all over again in less than a week?

I had to work through the weekend and when I got off my mother picked me up and we searched the best we could. We searched the whole weekend. I came up with nothing as Sunday night approached and I had to go to work. I started my shift. All the while, I thought that I was going back to prison because I couldn't find a place to live. I would lose my job and didn't know how long I would be incarcerated until my mother could find a place for me to go. I worked hard that night. Even though my spirit was down, I found strength and held fast to my faith and prayed. I prayed, "God, whatever your will is let it be done." I heard a gentle voice in my inner-self whisper to me, reminding me of a scripture. Matthew 14:31 "O thou of little faith, wherefore didst thou doubt?"

Almost immediately my doubt was comforted. Though I didn't know my fate, I had to trust God because this is what He has asked me to undertake. I was prepared to go to jail that morning. My shift was over and my mother waited outside for me. I got in the car and we rode to McDonald's to grab some breakfast as we headed to the parole office. The closer we got, the sadder my mom became until she was in tears. I grabbed her hand and said, "Mom we just got to trust in God and let whatever happens happen. I looked hard for a place to stay and we came up with nothing, so I'm prepared to go to jail until you find something." I repeated what I heard in my spirit and the scripture. She was still crying but she was comforted by my approach. I was the first one at the parole office that morning. I sat in the lobby waiting on my parole officer to come out and get me as my mother sat beside me holding clenching my hand.

The chief parole officer came out and called my name and invited us into his office. I walked in notknowing what to expect but had a feeling that I was going back to jail.

When I sat down, the chief said, "Who told you that you were going back to prison?

I said, "My parole officer told me Friday if I didn't find a place to go, you were sending me to jail 'til I find a place to live."

He said, "Well, I got strange phone call from my boss, the chairman of the parole board, asking me who threatened to send you to prison. I told him it wasn't me, but I'll find out what's going on." He followed with, "The chairman said, we made a mistake in his release and we will fix it. He is not going back to jail, he will continue his life." The chief went on to say, "I never said that and until you hear it from my mouth you are ok. You keep doing a great job and enjoy your life. Have a great day and congratulations on your release."

All I could do was smile and walk out to my mom. I grabbed her hand and rushed out the door and told her everything that just happened. We both rejoiced. I finally could feel some comfort and not the threat of going back to prison. The next couple of weeks were exciting even though I didn't like where I was staying. Yet it was December and I was able to spend time with my family for the first time in 15 years on Christmas. I gave my son and my mom some money and I enjoyed the holidays.

January 2008 came and it was amazing to be out. The world never looked so big before. Andrea called me one day and asked "Are you looking for a car?"

I said, "Yes."

She said, "Well I want to sell you my Jeep Cherokee if you want it."

I said, "Yes I do!"

She said, "Well let's make the arrangements." Within a couple of days, I had my first car since 1992. I was like a kid with a new toy and yes, I was glad to be riding and not walking. I thanked God for Andrea and my $1500 Cherokee!

A few months passed by and, I must say, I was enjoying myself, being free. I was being requested to come speak at schools and churches concerning my life in prison. Everything was good, yet there were still some embarrassing moments because I always felt I needed to be honest with people about my life and even telling them about being placed on the sex offender registry. I was enjoying going up to my son's school to pick him up. I even enrolled in school for heating and air tech. I was really enjoying going to school and then going to work. I loved the feeling of being responsible. But as the months went on, the sex offense topic kept rearing its head. The Offender Registry was a hot topic in the news and legislation. It seemed as if they were trying to get tougher, making it almost impossible to survive even though I didn't have a sex charge. I was told I couldn't speak at the Clayton Project HIP, which really hurt me. They feared someone would realize I was on the registry and stir something up.

One day, I received a phone call from the Southern Center of Human Rights. They were interested in representing me as well, as others who had similar issues concerning the sex offender registration law. I was kind of scared at first because I wasn't thrilled about being the poster boy for the law since I don't even have a sex offense charge. I thought about it for a few days and prayed hard about it. I finally made a decision to go with it because I wasn't only fighting for me, but everyone that was in the same situation.

The next several months were intense. I was in the newspaper and also featured on the local TV news channels. There were moments when people I knew recognized my face on the sex offender registry website. I was so embarrassed, but yet I had to let people know the truth because I was innocent. I wasn't a child molester. I also had to destroy the myth that when a person was on the sex offender registry list doesn't mean they are a child molester. When I walked into schools to speak or even visit my son, it felt horrible because I never wanted anyone to have those thoughts of me.

2009 came and the hard work of the Southern Center of Human Rights was rewarded with another victory. They were allowing some of us, that weren't labeled as a predators, to find housing and even keep our jobs. There were times when my very residence and job was in jeopardy. I had to weep to friends about maybe not having employment or even a place to live. But there was victory in 2009 and I was happy.

I had to testify in Federal Court. The D.A. didn't even have any substantial evidence to back up their claim of why some of us should even be on the registry list. I finally was able to get my own place and move out of the transitional home. I was still working for the battery company and trying to survive.

The year went on and it was October and things were going well. I ran into a young lady that told me she remembered when I came to her church and spoke and invited me back. I accepted the offer and went there the next Sunday. I walked into Springfield Baptist Church and went to the office area and sent a message to the senior pastor that I was part of the choir that came to his church back in 2007, when I was incarcerated, and that I was out now.

I went back to the sanctuary and some of the deacons sat me down in the front. The praise team sang, then the pastor came out and spoke. Before he went into his sermon, he invited me up to give my testimony. It felt good to be welcomed by the same congregation that welcomed me a couple years back. The pastor invited me to his office when church was over and we spoke for a while. He introduced me to Mr. Johnson who eventually helped me to get into DeKalb Technical College for HVAC. I couldn't finish my other degree because I was totally discouraged with all that was going on in my life. But this was a fresh start and I was excited.

In the latter part of October, I got the news that the battery company was doing away with 3$^{rd}$ shift. I got laid off from my job because they were downsizing. A couple of days later, Mrs. Nix called me and said Chaplin Nix passed away. I was devastated by this one-two blow.

Chaplain Nix was a true spiritual leader and a father figure to me. It hurt my soul that I could no longer talk with him and lean on him for guidance. He left a mark on me and I still remember the words he once told me. He said, "Omar, the mark of a man is one that wakes up every morning and is able to handle multiple crises." I didn't understand so he used his own life as an illustration. He said, "I have to be a father, a husband, a spiritual leader, an employee and so on without losing my mind. I have to balance it all." That was a solid statement that I still use when things are thrown at me.

While trying to figure out what I was going to do since I've been laid off, I applied for unemployment and started school on Nov 4, 2009. That same month, I got a call from my friend and sister, as I called her, Andrea. She had a proposition for me.

Andrea said, "We would like you to go back in as a chaplain."

I couldn't believe what I was hearing, plus there was no way would they allow me to go back in. I was a convicted felon. I was still on parole. Plus I hadn't beat the sex offender status yet. Andrea went on to say, "If you do, I need for you to take the volunteer certification and then we're going to set up a meeting with the superintendent of the Atlanta Transitional Center to see if you can take Chaplain Nix' spot."

I took the class a week later and set up a meeting with the superintendent. The day of the meeting, I went to the office to talk with him and I was expecting a no, or even a hell no, since I hadn't long been out of prison. I told him that I would like to take the position of chaplain now that there is a vacancy.

I was stunned with the response that he gave me. He said, "Omar, that's the best thing I've heard since Chaplain Nix died. I think that would be a good idea to bring you in since you know the ins and outs of my chaplain program and who better to put in position than someone who has been in prison, and now is out giving back to the community. I would love to have you as our Chaplain."

I was in awe of what he said. He called all his staff and said, "Omar Howard is our new chaplain. Bring him some keys and make him an ID. If anyone has a problem come talk to me directly."

This has never been done in the State of Georgia and maybe the country; to allow a person to come back in as a chaplain at the same place he paroled out from just 2 years before. Not to mention, still on parole for another year and a half! Unfortunately most of the officers didn't approve of it and even some of the volunteers. I was to start my position in January of 2010.

On December 4, 2009, I went to court to see if I would be removed from the Sex Offender Registry. It had been a long 2 year battle, with a couple of victories in between, that lead up to us being able to file to be removed. I was anxious to go to court to settle this dispute.

December 3, 2009, the day before I had to go to court, I was awakened by a telephone call from my attorney. I was half asleep when she said, "I have some good news! You don't have to go to court tomorrow. The judge signed off on your petition and you are no longer on the sex offender list. I will send all your signed paperwork to the proper authorities so you can be taken off the website. Congratulations!"

I rolled out of bed and hit the ground in excitement. It was done! She said it Judge Adams signed off. I couldn't believe what I had just heard. The judge that signed off on my petition was also the DA on the 1993 murder charge that I was currently on parole for and had served 15 years for that crime. I was so excited to call my mom and tell her the good news. All I think was, "God you have done some amazing things!"

I started as the chaplain of The Atlanta Transitional Center in January, 2010. I must say, it was awesome being a testament to the guys who attended services and came to events we provided. My name spread through the system. I received letters from guys that I used to be locked-up with. Some, I considered friends and others that didn't wish me any good when I was incarcerated, but it was amazing to see how guys reached out to congratulate me, and of course, ask if I can help them in some way. That didn't bother me. I actually enjoyed the response because those guys knew that

I wasn't doing this for show. If anything, I was able to inspire them to persevere and never give up pushing.

Since my release, I've constantly tried to evolve, adapt and continue to mature, but it hasn't come without its difficulties. I learned quickly that I was still somewhat institutionalized. Being deprived of freedom for so long that no amount of training will make life in the outside world easy. Being an only child, I liked to be to myself even though I'm very sociable when I'm involved in the community. Financial choices, learning how important your credit rating is, how to date, how to love, how to pick yourself back up after a failed relationship. The challenge of being out of prison, after serving a long term, was that I went in prison as an 18 year old kid and when I got out, I was still an 18 year old kid in a 33 year old body. The biggest challenge of becoming a mature, responsible man, was the fact I didn't know how to be one.

After a decade, I still struggle in so many ways because I never had a blueprint of what a man was supposed to be, or how to act. The constant reality is I'm a convicted felon with serious charges, with a past, that hinders me from certain jobs and living areas.

The two things that that keep me pushing are my continuing desire to seek God's will and a fierce determination to be successful. There have been a lot of sacrifices, but the determination to survive in this big world fuels me. I have started a mentoring program that keeps me grounded. I humbly give countless hours to helping at risk youth.

I've learned some valuable lessons over the decade of being a free man and I'm willing to keep pushing to get better. Asked if I had to do it all over again to become the man I am today, I probably would say, yes. I would take advantage of all the things I took for granted in my life, with the hope that I could still have the passion to serve and help others. My life has been the ultimate challenge when it comes to manhood and I'm still learning.

If I didn't learn anything else, I've learned this one thing...

Freedom is a Choice and I Choose Freedom!

# ABOUT THE AUTHOR

## OMAR HOWARD

*Mr. Omar Howard of Stone Mountain, GA, the founder of Freedom is A Choice Inc., is a successful individual with an incarcerated history. He used his previous incarceration as a tool to counsel and mentor at-risk youth and troubled adults to make choices that will impact the rest of their lives.*

*Omar was granted parole in 2007 and released on December 10th of that year. Though there were many legal and personal obstacles to come, Omar persevered through some tough times that would have caused most individuals to give up but, his passion to serve and help others pushed him to strive for success.*

*Since being released from prison after serving 14 years, 10 months, Omar has volunteered for HeartBound Ministries, and now serves as the chaplain at the Atlanta Transitional Center, an opportunity that has never been allowed in the history of the Georgia Department of Corrections especially to a convicted felon who had just 2 years before been released from that facility.*

*His successful transition from prison to society serves as a positive example to at-risk and troubled youth throughout the state to choose freedom over incarceration. Omar decided to further his education by completing and graduating as a HVAC Technician from Dekalb Technical College, also having certifications for Anger Management specialist and The Integrity Project.*

*Mr. Howard has appeared on several television and radio broadcasts. The Atlanta Journal-Constitution, and other local newspapers, have featured numerous articles about his positive journey. Omar travels Georgia speaking to schools, colleges, prison, youth events, and facilitating his own youth forums. Omar has been awarded for The President's Volunteer Service Award from President Barack Obama and was also awarded The Non-profit Trinity Award for Outstanding Volunteer Service. He has partnered with The Department of Justice, The U.S Attorney's Office and The Department of Juvenile Justice to be a mentor and a public speaker.*

*Omar's passion to serve our community in a positive way has helped a number of young people make better life choices and decisions. Omar has started his own non-profit organization called Freedom is a Choice, Inc. which is geared toward encouraging our youth to choose freedom over incarceration and with perseverance and God's strength, he will continue to use Freedom is a Choice as his life, passion, and message.*

*Omar has been blessed to have received a Pardon from Georgia State Board of Pardons and Paroles.*

## STATE BOARD OF PARDONS AND PAROLES

## PARDON

WHEREAS, Omar Sheehan Howard , Serial Number EF-316762 was convicted in the court(s) indicated below of the following offense(s) for which he/she received the sentence(s) hereinafter set forth:

| OFFENSE | COURT OF CONVICTION | DATE SENTENCE BEGAN | SENTENCE |
|---|---|---|---|
| Armed Robbery (3cts), Aggravated Assault (3cts), False Imprisonment (3cts), Possession of F/A during Felony (3cts), Possession of F/A by 1st offender (93CR2090) | DeKalb Superior | 7/23/1993 | 10 years to serve cc on Cts 1-6, 5 years to serve cc on Ct 7, 5 years to serve cc on cts 8-10, 5 years to serve cc on ct 11, Closed: 4/21/2011 |
| Voluntary Manslaughter (93CR2911) | DeKalb Superior | 11/22/1993 | 18 years to serve, Closed: 4/21/2011 |

and,

WHEREAS, an application for a Pardon has been filed by the above named individual; and

WHEREAS, having investigated the facts material to the pardon application, which investigation has established to the satisfaction of the Board that the pardon applicant has been crime free for six years, maintained continuous employment, made educational improvements, is a law-abiding citizen and is fully rehabilitated;

THEREFORE, pursuant to Article IV, Section II, Paragraph II (a), of the Constitution of the State of Georgia, the Board, without implying innocence, hereby unconditionally fully pardons said individual, and it is hereby

ORDERED that all disabilities under Georgia law resulting from the above stated conviction (s) and sentence (s), as well as, any other Georgia conviction (s) and sentence(s) imposed prior thereto, be and each and all are hereby removed; and

ORDERED FURTHER that all civil and political rights, except the right to receive, possess, or transport in commerce a firearm, lost under Georgia law as a result of the above stated conviction(s) and sentence(s), as well as, any other Georgia conviction(s) and sentence(s) imposed prior thereto, be and each and all are hereby restored.

It is directed that copies of this order be furnished to the said applicant and to the Clerk(s) of Court(s) in the County(s) where the above sentence(s) were imposed.

GIVEN UNDER THE HAND AND SEAL of the State Board of Pardons and Paroles, this 24th day of January, 2018.

STATE BOARD OF PARDONS AND PAROLES

*Caryl Deems*

FOR THE BOARD
Caryl Deems

# Choices and Consequences

## Reading Comprehension Assessment

### Evasive Thinking / Critical Thinking

# Choices and Consequences

## Reading Comprehension Assessment
## Evasive Thinking / Critical Thinking

1. Give some specific examples of hardships Omar Howard went through when he was growing up.


2. What choices could he have made as a little kid that would have caused him to be a better teenager?

3. When a family friend violated him, what should he have done? Who should he have told?




4. When Omar Howard was a teen, what choices could he have made differently?

5. Did Omar Howard do the right thing by not telling the truth? If he told the truth, what response would he face from his friends?

6. Pick a specific situation Omar Howard was in and explain what you would have done differently.

7. Do the choices you make only affect you? Explain how they affect your family and community

8. Have you ever been in a situation that you knew was wrong or illegal?
If yes, choose one instance and explain how you handled it (no names please).

What would you do now or in the future to handle the situation differently?

9. Do you have a problem saying "No" to a situation you know is wrong or illegal? If yes, what prevents you from saying "No"?

10. Do you associate with people that you know are making bad choices?

   If yes, do you still hang around them?

   If no, how do you handle it when you meet new people that seem to be making bad choices?

11. Are there people in your life that you respect that make it difficult for you to distance yourself from illegal activity because of how they would feel?

   If yes, have you ever thought of some ways to start distancing yourself? If not, why?

12. Are you concerned about how others will perceive you if you began to make better decisions? If so, why?

13. How well do you know the law? Do you know the consequences if you break certain laws?

14. Have you Googled specific offenses to see how much time you could serve for breaking specific laws?

15. Is committing crime for financial gain worth going to prison or losing your life? Please explain.

16. Do you take education seriously or is it just something you are required to do? How do you plan to finish your education?

17. What are some of your life goals? Do you think that you can achieve them? Why or why not?

This assessment is designed for you to thinking about the choices you make by analyzing the behavior of the author and your behavior as we are challenge everyday of our lives to make critical and evasive thinking that will hopefully keep us out of jail or even worst.

- Author Omar Howard

Made in the USA
Middletown, DE
29 June 2023

34207556R00096